Also by Gary Soucie

Hook, Line, and Sinker

SOUCIE'S FIELD GUIDE OF FISHING FACTS

by Gary Soucie

A FIRESIDE BOOK
Published by Simon & Schuster Inc.
NEW YORK LONDON TORONTO SYDNEY TOKYO

First Fireside Edition, 1988

Published by the Simon & Schuster Trade Division
by arrangement with Nick Lyons Books

Simon & Schuster Building
Rockefeller Center
1230 Avenue of the Americas
New York, New York 10020

Originally entitled *Soucie's Fishing Data Book*
FIRESIDE and colophon are registered trademarks
of Simon & Schuster Inc.

Designed by Stanley S. Drate/Folio Graphics Co. Inc.
Manufactured in the United States of America

10 9 8 7 6 5 4 3 2 1 Pbk.

Library of Congress Cataloging in Publication Data

Soucie, Gary.
    [Fishing data book]
    Soucie's field guide of fishing facts / Gary Soucie. — 1st
Fireside ed.
        p.   cm.
    A Fireside Book.
    Reprint. Originally published: Soucie's fishing data book.
Piscataway, N.J. : Winchester Press, c1985
    Includes index.
    ISBN 0-671-66645-2 Pbk.
    1. Fishing—Handbooks. manuals, etc.   I. Title.   II. Title: Field
guide of fishing facts.
SH441.S744 1988
799.1'2—dc19   88-11386
                                                           CIP

CONTENTS

PREFACE

The world of outdoor journalism has historically been dominated by what are called me-'n'-Joe stories, short for me-'n'-Joe-went-fishin' stories. Editors pretend not to like them, and "We don't buy me-'n'-Joe stories" has become the anthem of outdoor publishing. But the very best of outdoor writing has always been and will probably continue to be in this vein—and for good reason. Fishing is a very personal thing. Even most fishing information of the sort people plug into how-to stories is of a subjective, experiential, anecdotal nature.

But there is a body of objective information about fish and fishing. Trouble is, you never can find it when you need it; at least I can't. In fact, I probably wrote this book as much for myself as for you.

If you have a very big fishing library, chances are good that you already have on your bookshelves most of the information I have gathered together for this book. But, I'd like to think, it isn't so well organized, or so easy to find and use.

I have organized the information so that you can analyze it and decide which bits and pieces of it can help you to improve your fishing. It won't, I promise you, all be equally useful. If you never fish salt water, you won't have much use for information on bluewater trolling patterns or the temperature preferences of billfish. And if you are a Pacific Northwest steelhead specialist, the temperature preferences of bowfin or the spawning seasons of bluefish will be just so much applesauce. But, I can almost guarantee, no matter where you live or how you fish, you will find information in here that you can use. Analyze it according to your needs and make your own decisions as to its timely application, and you will catch more fish. And have more fun in the bargain.

A few caveats and footnotes are in order.

Angling facts, especially of the numerical variety, aren't so reliable as, say, vector analyses on engineering drawings. For one thing, fish are living creatures, subject to all the vagaries and influences of genetics and environment. Behavior, growth, everything else about them, is subject to variation from the norm. In one stretch of river on a single day, I have caught rainbow trout that varied in color from pale silvery gray to outrageously rosy patterns. Some came in like clumps of moss, some jumped several times, others kept darting back and forth in search of a safe haven in the rocks. I have watched two anglers of similar experience, using identical tackle, stand shoulder to shoulder as they battled almost identical-twin little tunny. One brought his fish to gaff with efficient dispatch, while the other watched his twelve-pound fish make repeated runs against a fifty-pound trolling outfit's drag. You can't blame the fish; they haven't read the books.

Then you must consider the source. I should have said, "sources," for they are many and diverse. Sometimes the information came from scientists who may fish only with seines and traps. Sometimes it came from fishermen and fishing writers who are longer on skill and experience than on the empirical method of data gathering, reduction, and analysis. And sometimes it came from tackle companies and other manufacturers and importers who have commercial axes to grind.

I have had to gather facts and information from a wide variety of sources, whose methods and purposes varied a great deal. And sometimes I've had to wrestle the data to serve a practical sport-fishing purpose the researcher certainly never anticipated or intended. Most scientists are extremely precise in the way they collect and list data, so accuracy isn't a problem. But applicability is, because a conservative scientist can be so precise and narrow that it's very difficult to apply his findings to another season, another year, another body of water. Tackle companies may or may not be precise, and they may handle their numbers conservatively or liberally. Funny things sometimes happen to facts on their way from the research labs to the marketing and advertising departments.

All the information I have gathered should be measured against your own experience. Don't hesitate to call me wrong when you have gathered information that is contradictory. But don't be too sure that your data—gathered under less than ideal conditions, in only a few places, and at odd times here and there—is more generally applicable. The body of factual fishing information grows fitfully, in tiny bits and big chunks, slowly here and rapidly there. Its growth may not be orderly, but it grows.

Think what it might be like, in this crowded and polluted world, if we knew as little about fish and fishing as our forebears did when the waters fairly teemed with fish.

FISH

Where else to begin, but with fish? Everything else, the tackle, the techniques, the tips and tricks, exists only to serve our need to get closer to those fish. It doesn't make any difference where or how you fish, whether you spend a lot or a little time and money on the sport, it all revolves around fish. Whether you fish for a small number of species or will settle for anything that swims, you will never know too much about the creatures you stalk. The more you learn about fish, the more fun you will have, whether you are an aesthetically inclined fly caster, a boat-loving troller, a restless prowler of backcountry bays and bayous, or a bankside devotee of *il dolce far niente*.

A lot of what we need to know about fish does not lend itself well to consideration as data. And some of what does—the pH preferences of freshwater fish, for example—has not yet been thoroughly enough studied for inclusion here. But there is plenty of information to chew on, from the temperatures that trigger feeding or spawning to the hazards of handling certain species.

To make it easier to find fish in some of the tables that follow, I have separated freshwater from saltwater species, and sportfish from baitfish. Some fish belong in more than one category. In deciding where to place a fish, I have used the following criteria: (1) If the species is both fished for sport and used for bait, I have

chosen to honor it as a sportfish, unless its sporting status is incidental compared to its overwhelming use as bait; in cases of
doubt, I have almost always opted for listing it as a sportfish. (2)
When a fish occurs in both fresh and salt water, I have placed it
where I think most anglers fish for it; but if a species is almost
equally popular in fresh and salt water, sometimes I have decided
to list it in both places.

PREFERRED WATER TEMPERATURES

Being coldblooded animals, fish must rely upon the temperature
of the water in which they live to regulate their own body temperatures and body processes. So, in any given body of water, there
may be a lot of water that is absolutely devoid of the species you
are after. In still waters, temperature is largely a function of
depth. But it may also be a function of shade, springs, waterfalls,
tributary inflows. In flowing waters, these other factors may be
more important than depth, especially the influx of colder water
from tributaries or spring sources.

In all bodies of water, fish may enter water of temperatures that
are outside the listed range, and for a variety of reasons. They
may have gotten there by following prey or been chased there by
predators. In the ocean, they might have got caught up in an eddy
of water that broke away from a warm current and then eventually
cooled down. Even in lakes, fish may find good habitat that is an
acceptable water temperature immediately after the spring thaw;
yet, later in the season, there may be areas of better water temperature elsewhere but that are separated from where the fish are
concentrated by water that is too hot or too cold to encourage
traveling.

In some cases, water temperature is not so important as other
factors. Trout and salmon are thought to be very temperature-
dependent, but in fact the concentration of dissolved oxygen may
be a more important consideration. Salmonids and other so-called
cold-water species thrive best in water where oxygen concentra-
tions are near saturation. All other things being equal (and they
almost never are), the colder the water, the more oxygen it will
hold when saturated. This is so because the solubility of oxygen in
water decreases as the temperature rises.

However, if you can find water of the right temperature (assuming that habitat, pH, dissolved oxygen levels, water clarity, and other factors are within reason), chances are you will find fish.

Caveat piscator: Important as water temperature is, the situation is rather confusing when it comes to the available data. Whether the temperature ranges you see published in books and magazine articles came from fishermen or scientists, they suffer from having been taken over limited periods of time in limited numbers of locations. They may or may not be applicable in other years or other waters. Given any range of temperatures, you might reasonably ask whether it represents ideal, optimum, preferred, or merely tolerable temperatures. Unfortunately, the originators of the numbers are never around to answer.

In the table that follows, I have listed the best temperature data I can find. In some cases, the numbers represent optimum temperatures for a species. In other cases, they more nearly represent the minimum and maximum temperatures within which a species might logically be expected to occur. It isn't possible to categorize each set of temperatures, but it is fairly safe to assume that the narrower the span, the more likely it represents some sort of optimum temperature range. If the two numbers are very far apart, they probably represent avoidance temperatures. For intervals that are neither very wide nor very narrow, they might represent feeding or activity ranges or general temperature preferences.

PREFERRED WATER TEMPERATURES

Freshwater Sportfish	Temperature (Degrees F)
ALEWIFE, *Alosa pseudoharengus*	54–70
BASS, LARGEMOUTH, *Micropterus salmoides*	80–82
BASS, ROCK, *Ambloplites rupestris*	70
BASS, SMALLMOUTH, *Micropterus dolomieu*	65–73
BASS SPOTTED, *Micropterus punctulatus*	70–78
BASS, STRIPED, *Morone saxatilis*	65–70
BASS, WHITE, *Morone chrysops*	66–75
BASS, WHITEROCK, *M. saxatalis* × *M. chrysops*	70s
BASS, YELLOW, *Morone mississippiensis*	80–81
BLOATER, *Coregonus hoyi*	38–45
BLUEGILL, *Lepomis macrochirus*	69–85+
BOWFIN, *Amia calva*	65+
BUFFALO, BIGMOUTH, *Ictiobus cyprinellus*	81–90
BULLHEAD, BLACK, *Ictalurus melas*	70–80+

Freshwater Sportfish	Temperature (Degrees F)
BULLHEAD, BROWN, *Ictalurus nebulosus*	74–78
BULLHEAD, YELLOW, *Ictalurus natalis*	83
BURBOT, *Lota lota*	50–65
CARP, COMMON, *Cyprinus carpio*	79–84
CARPSUCKERS, *Carpiodes spp.*	80–90
CATFISH, CHANNEL, *Ictalurus punctatus*	70–87
CATFISH, FLATHEAD, *Pylodictis olivaris*	82–88
CHAR, ARCTIC, *Salvelinus alpinus*	53–61
CISCO, *Coregonus artedii*	52–55
CRAPPIE, BLACK, *Pomoxis nigromaculatus*	70–75
CRAPPIE, WHITE, *Pomoxis annularis*	61–71
DRUM, FRESHWATER, *Aplodinotus grunniens*	74
FALLFISH, *Semotilus corporatus*	70s
GAR, LONGNOSE, *Lepisosteus osseus*	92
GAR, SHORTNOSE, *Lepisosteus platostomus*	82–92
GOLDEYE, *Hiodon alosoides*	70+
GRAYLING, ARCTIC, *Thymallus arcticus*	47–52
KOKANEE, *Oncorhynchus nerka*	50–59
MOONEYE, *Hiodon tergisus*	72–81
MUSKELLUNGE, *Esox masquinongy*	63–78
PERCH, WHITE, *Morone americana*	75–85
PERCH, YELLOW, *Perca flavescens*	66–77
PICKEREL, CHAIN, *Esox niger*	66–80
PICKEREL, GRASS, *Esox americanus vermiculatus*	78
PIKE, NORTHERN, *Esox lucius*	55–65
PUMPKINSEED, *Lepomis gibbosus*	82
QUILLBACK, *Carpiodes cyprinus*	72
REDHORSE, NORTHERN, *Maxostoma macrolepidotum*	73–80
SALMON, ATLANTIC, *Salmo salar*	50–62
SALMON, CHINOOK, *Oncorhynchus tshawytscha*	50–63
SALMON, CHUM, *Oncorhynchus keta*	48–57
SALMON, COHO, *Oncorhynchus kisutch*	44–57
SALMON, LANDLOCKED, *Salmo salar*	45–58
SALMON, PINK, *Oncorhynchus gorbuscha*	49–57
SALMON, SOCKEYE, *Oncorhynchus nerka*	50–59
SAUGER, *Stizostedion canadense*	66–67
SHAD, AMERICAN, *Alosa sapidissima*	59–70
SMELT, RAINBOW, *Osmerus mordax*	40–50
SPLAKE, *S. alvelinus fontinalis* × *S. namaycush*	54
STEELHEAD, *Salmo gairdneri*	48–52
STURGEON, ATLANTIC, *Acipenser oxyrhynchus*	66
STURGEON, WHITE, *Acipenser transmontanus*	63–64
SUCKER, LONGNOSE, *Catostomus catostomus*	53–65
SUCKER, WHITE, *Catostomus commersoni*	66–72
SUNFISH, GREEN, *Lepomis cyanellus*	87

Freshwater Sportfish	Temperature (Degrees F)
SUNFISHES, *Lepomis & Enneacanthus spp*	55–80
TENCH, *Tinca tinca*	Below 79
TROUT, BROOK, *Salvelinus fontinalis*	45–61
TROUT, BROWN, *Salmo trutta*	56–65
TROUT, CUTTHROAT, *Salmo clarki*	50–65
TROUT, GOLDEN, *Salmo aguabonita*	50–60
TROUT, LAKE, *Salvelinus namaycush*	40–55
TROUT, RAINBOW, *Salmo gairdneri*	50–70
WALLEYE, *Stizostedion vitreum*	59–68
WHITEFISH, LAKE, *Coregonus clupeaformis*	Below 51
WHITEFISH, MOUNTAIN, *Prosopium williamsoni*	48–52
WHITEFISH, ROUND, *Prosopium cylindraceum*	63

Freshwater Baitfish	Temperature (Degrees F)
BITTERLING, *Rhodeus sericeus*	77
CHUB, BLUEHEAD, *Hybopsis leptocephala*	59
CHUB, LAKE, *Couesius plumbeus*	45–55
DACE, NORTHERN REDBELLY, *Chrosomus eos*	70
GOLDFISH, *Carassius auratus*	77
HOG SUCKER, NORTHERN, *Hypentelium nigricans*	50+
KILLIFISHES, *Cyprinodontidae*	85
MINNOW, BLUNTNOSE, *Pimephales notatus*	84
MINNOW, FATHEAD, *Pimephales promelas*	84
MOSQUITOFISH, *Gambusia affinis*	81–85
MUDMINNOWS, *Umbra spp.*	55–84
MUDSUCKER, LONGJAW, *Gillichthys mirabilis*	72
SCULPINS, *Cottidae*	45–55
SHAD, GIZZARD, *Dorosoma cepedianum*	63–80
SHAD, THREADFIN, *Dorosoma petenense*	50–55
SHINER, COMMON, *Notropis cornutus*	65–83
SHINER, EMERALD, *Notropis atherinoides*	61–72
SHINER, GOLDEN, *Notemigonus crysoleucas*	70
SHINER, SPOTFIN, *Notropis spilopterus*	80s
SHINER, SPOTTAIL, *Notropis hudsonius*	54
STONECAT, *Notorus flavus*	59
STONEROLLER, *Campostoma anomalum*	84
SUCKER, MOUNTAIN, *Catostomus platyrhynchus*	60–74
TROUT-PERCH, *Percopsis omiscomaycus*	55–60

Saltwater Sportfish	Temperature (Degrees F)
ALBACORE, *Thunnus alalunga*	61–80
AMBERJACK, GREATER, *Seriola dumerili*	65–80
BARRACUDA, GREAT, *Sphyraena barracuda*	75–82
BASS, BLACK SEA, *Centropristis striata*	55–68
BASS, GIANT SEA, *Stereolepis gigas*	65–78
BASS, KELP, *Paralabrax clathratus*	65
BASS, STRIPED, *Morone saxatilis*	56–77
BLUEFISH, *Pomatomus saltatrix*	64–75
BONEFISH, *Albula vulpes*	75–88
BONITO, ATLANTIC, *Sarda sarda*	65–76
BONITO, PACIFIC, *Sarda chiliensis*	58–76
CATFISH, GAFFTOPSAIL, *Bagre marinus*	68–95
CATFISH, HARDHEAD, *Arius felis*	77–99
CERO, *Scomberomorus regalis*	70–80
COBIA, *Rachycentron canadum*	68–86
COD, ATLANTIC, *Gadus morhua*	44–58
CROAKER, ATLANTIC, *Micropogon undulatus*	61+
CUSK, *Brosme brosme*	41–46
DOGFISH, SMOOTH, *Mustelus canis*	50–59
DOGFISH, SPINY, *Squalus acanthias*	46–54
DOLPHIN, *Coryphaena hippurus*	78–85
DRUM, BLACK, *Pogonias cromis*	56–80
DRUM, RED, *Sciaenops ocellatus*	56–84
FLOUNDER, SMOOTH, *Liopsetta putnami*	30–60
FLOUNDER, SUMMER, *Paralichthys dentatus*	65–72
FLOUNDER, WINTER, *Pseudopleuronectes americanus*	53–60
GOOSEFISH, *Lophius americanus*	32–70
GRUNION, CALIFORNIA, *Leuresthes tenuis*	77
HADDOCK, *Melanogrammus aeglefinus*	45–52
HAKE, RED, *Urophycis chuss*	40–50
HAKE, SILVER, *Merluccius bilinearis*	40–59
HAKE, WHITE, *Urophycis tenuis*	39–48
HALIBUT, ATLANTIC, *Hippoglossus hippoglossus*	37–48
HAMMERHEAD, SCALLOPED, *Sphyrna lewini*	62–86
HAMMERHEAD, SMOOTH, *Sphyrna zygaena*	67+
JACK, CREVALLE, *Caranx hippos*	70–80
JACKSMELT, *Atherinops californiensis*	77
JEWFISH, *Epinephelus itajara*	72–88
KAWAKAWA, *Euthynnus affinis*	60–88
KINGFISH, NORTHERN, *Menticirrhus saxatalis*	46+
KINGFISH, SOUTHERN, *Menticirrhus americanus*	50+
MACKEREL, ATLANTIC, *Scomber scombrus*	45–68
MACKEREL, KING, *Scomberomorus cavalla*	70–75
MACKEREL, SPANISH, *Scomberomorus maculatus*	67+
MAKO, SHORTFIN, *Isurus oxyrinchus*	64–70

Saltwater Sportfish	Temperature (Degrees F)
MARLIN, BLACK, *Makaira indica*	75–85
MARLIN, BLUE, *Makaira nigricans*	70–88
MARLIN STRIPED, *Tetrapturus audax*	65–80
MARLIN, WHITE, *Tetrapturus alba*	70–85
OPALEYE, *Girella nigricans*	79
PERCH, OCEAN, *Sebastes marinus*	32–60
PERCH, WHITE, *Morone americana*	60s–80s
PERMIT, *Trachinotus falcatus*	72–84
POLLOCK, *Pollachius virens*	45–60
POMPANO, FLORIDA, *Trachinotus carolinus*	70–86
ROOSTERFISH, *Nematistius pectoralis*	68–85
RUNNER, RAINBOW, *Elegatis bipinnulata*	70–85
SAILFISH, *Istiophorus platypterus*	75–85
SCUP, *Stenotomus chrysops*	45+
SEABASS, WHITE, *Atractoscion nobilis*	68
SEATROUT, SPOTTED, *Cynoscion nebulosus*	65–75
SHARK, BLUE, *Prionace glauca*	50–68
SHARK, DUSKY, *Carcharhinus obscurus*	73+
SHARK PORBEAGLE, *Lamna nasus*	40–60
SHARK, SANDBAR, *Carcharhinus plumbeus*	74+
SHARK, SILKY, *Carcharhinus falciformis*	76–84
SHARK, THRESHER, *Alopias vulpinus*	60–75
SHARK, TIGER, *Galeocerdo cuvieri*	55–85
SHARK, WHITE, *Carcharodon carcharias*	50–84
SMELT, RAINBOW, *Osmerus mordax*	Below 59
SNAPPER, RED, *Lutjanus campechanus*	57–60
SNOOK, *Centropomus undecimalis*	70–86
SWORDFISH, *Xiphias gladius*	58–70
TARPON, *Megalops atlanticus*	74–88
TAUTOG, *Tautoga onitis*	46–70
TOPSMELT, *Atherinops affinis*	77
TREVALLY, GIANT, *Caranx ignobilis*	70–88
TUNA, BIGEYE, *Thunnus obesus*	60–75
TUNA, BLACKFIN, *Thunnus atlanticus*	70–82
TUNA, BLUEFIN, *Thunnus thynnus*	56–84
TUNA, SKIPJACK, *Euthynnus pelamis*	67–78
TUNA, YELLOWFIN, *Thunnus albacares*	64–80
TUNNY, LITTLE, *Euthynnus alletteratus*	65+
WAHOO, *Acanthocybium solanderi*	70–86
WEAKFISH, *Cynoscion regalis*	55–70
WOLFFISH, ATLANTIC, *Anarhichas lupus*	31–52
YELLOWTAIL, CALIFORNIA, *Seriola lalandei dorsalis*	60–80

Saltwater Baitfish	Temperature (Degrees F)
ANCHOVY, BAY, *Anchoa mitchilli*	82
ANCHOVY, STRIPED, *Anchoa hepsetus*	59–95
BALAO, *Hemiramphus balao*	70–80
BALLYHOO, *Hemiramphus brasiliensis*	70s
HERRING, ATLANTIC, *Clupea harengus harengus*	53–89
HERRING, SKIPJACK, *Alosa chrysochloris*	75–80
MENHADEN, ATLANTIC, *Brevoortia tyrannus*	66–96
SILVERSIDE, ATLANTIC, *Menidia menidia*	64–77

SPAWNING SEASONS AND TEMPERATURES

Because the spawning runs or movements of fish may affect their availability to anglers in a given location, knowing at least a little about the reproductive part of a fish's life cycle may be crucial to angling success. This tends to be more important when angling for freshwater or anadromous species than for saltwater species. Water temperature seems to be an important spawning "trigger" for many freshwater and anadromous species, but it apparently is not very important for most saltwater fish. Some fish are rather predictable in their spawning responses to environmental and other conditions, whereas others appear to be erratic. In many cases, local populations of fish may behave differently from other populations of the same species. So, if you are going to study the spawning movements of your quarry, you had better be more precise than I can afford to be in a general book like this. Even so, the information that follows may help to explain what otherwise looks like a random pattern of success and failure in your fishing.

Warning: Several states prohibit the taking of certain species during their spawning seasons, a laudable restriction. Unfortunately, this aspect of fisheries management hasn't yet become very widespread. I suspect we'll someday rue our having allowed the taking of fish on their spawning beds or during the spawning runs, either commercially or for sport. In the case of shad, salmon, and too many other species, fishing pressure is concentrated almost entirely on the spawning periods. I think sportfishing would be better served if anglers used information on spawning seasons and temperatures to avoid taking spawning fish, rather than targeting them during their reproductive season. No matter where you stand on this issue, be sure to check local fishing laws before taking sport or bait species during their spawning periods.

Some of the spawning seasons listed in the chart below span periods of several months. Most of the time, this represents different spawning periods in different parts of the fish's range. Individual fish or local populations within a given species may also exhibit different spawning responses to water temperatures. Sometimes, it is because water temperature is not so important in determining spawning movements as such other factors as water chemistry, turbidity, salinity, or the like. And sometimes it's that fish acclimated to different temperatures may have different thermal triggers when it comes to spawning. Again, I have tried to give ranges of temperatures and, when feasible, to identify in **bold face** the temperatures that tend to determine peak spawning activity.

In all cases, remember that spawning runs may not immediately precede spawning periods. Most Atlantic salmon, for example, actually spawn in October or November, yet fish may begin entering rivers as early as January or as late as October. The information in the accompanying chart cannot take the place of careful observation and study on the part of the individual angler.

The three-letter abbreviations of the months and seasons probably require no explanation, but know that "YR" stands for year-round, "E" for early, and "L" for late. "Jan–Sep" means that spawning occurs more or less continuously (considering all the different populations throughout the range of the species) from January through September. "**May–Jun; F**" indicates that there are two distinct spawning periods, the major one in May and June, and a lesser one in the fall.

SPAWNING SEASONS AND TEMPERATURES

Freshwater Sportfish	Temperature (Degrees F) Low/Peak/Hi	Spawning Season
BASS, LARGEMOUTH, *Micropterus salmoides*	60/**62–65**/80	May-**Jun**-Aug
BASS, REDEYE, *Micropterus coosae*		May-Jul
BASS, ROCK, *Ambloplites rupestris*	60/ /70	May-Jun
BASS, SMALLMOUTH, *Micropterus dolomieu*	55/**61–65**/70	Apr-Jul
BASS, SPOTTED, *Micropterus punctulatus*	**64–68**	May-Jul
BASS, STRIPED, *Morone saxatilis*	55–67	Apr-May
BASS SUWANEE, *Micropterus notius*		Feb-Jun

Freshwater Sportfish	Temperature (Degrees F) Low/Peak/Hi	Spawning Season
BASS, WHITE, *Morone chrysops*	55/58–60/70	Apr-Jun
BASS, YELLOW, *Morone mississippiensis*	/70	Apr-May
BLOATER, *Coregonus hoyi*		**Feb-Mar**;YR
BLUEGILL, *Lepomis macrochirus*	50/60–65/70	May-Aug
BOWFIN, *Amia calva*	61–66	**Apr-May**
BUFFALO, BIGMOUTH, *Ictiobus cyprinellus*	60–65	May-Jun
BUFFALO, SMALLMOUTH, *Ictiobus bubalis*	59/60–70/81	Mar-**Jul**-Sep
BULLHEAD, BLACK, *Ictalurus melas*	63/70+	May-Jul
BULLHEAD, BROWN, *Ictalurus nebulosus*	70/	May-Jun
BULLHEAD, YELLOW, *Ictalurus natalis*		May-Jun
BURBOT, *Lota lota*	33–35	Nov-May
CARP, COMMON, *Cyprinus carpio*	59/65–68/82	Jun
CARPSUCKERS, *Carpiodes spp.*	60	Apr-Jun
CATFISH, CHANNEL, *Ictalurus punctatus*	71/80/85	Mar-**Jun**-Jul
CATFISH, FLATHEAD, *Pylodictis olivaris*		May-Jul
CATFISH, WHITE, *Ictalurus catus*		Jun-Jul
CISCO, *Coregonus artedii*	34/38/41	Sep-Dec
CRAPPIE, BLACK, *Pomoxis nigromaculatus*	64–68	**May-Jun**-Aug
CRAPPIE, WHITE, *Pomoxis annularis*	57/61–68/73	May-**Jun**-Jul
DOLLY VARDEN, *Salvelinus malma*	42/44–46	Fall
DRUM, FRESHWATER, *Aplodinotus grunniens*		Apr-Sep
FLIER, *Centrarchus macropterus*	63	Mar-May
GAR, ALLIGATOR, *Lepisosteus spatula*	40/ /52	Apr-Jun
GAR, FLORIDA, *Lepisosteus platyrhincus*		**Apr-May**-Oct
GAR, LONGNOSE, *Lepisosteus osseus*		Mar-Aug
GAR, SHORTNOSE, *Lepisosteus platostomus*	66–74	May-Jul
GAR, SPOTTED, *Lepisosteus oculatus*		Spring
GOLDEYE, *Hiodon alosoides*	50–55	May-Jul
GRAYLING, ARCTIC, *Thymallus arcticus*	44–50	Apr-Jun
INCONNU, *Stenodus leucichthys*		May-Oct
KOKANEE, *Oncorhynchus nerka*	41/45/53	Aug-Apr
MOONEYE, *Hiodon tergisus*		Apr-Jun
MUSKELLUNGE, *Esox masquinongy*	49/55/59	Apr-May
PADDLEFISH, *Polyodon spathula*		Apr-May
PEAMOUTH, *Mylocheilus caurinus*	52/54/72	May-Jul
PERCH, PIRATE, *Aphredoderus sayanus*	61	Apr-Jun
PERCH, SACRAMENTO, *Archoplites interruptus*		May-Jun
PERCH, WHITE, *Morone americana*	64–70	Apr-Jun
PERCH, YELLOW, *Perca flavescens*	40/45–50/54	Apr-Jul
PICKEREL, CHAIN, *Esox niger*	47–52	**Apr-May**;F

Freshwater Sportfish	Temperature (Degrees F) Low/Peak/Hi	Spawning Season
PICKEREL, GRASS, *Esox americanus vermiculatus*	45/50–53	Mar-May;F
PICKEREL, REDFIN, *Esox americanus americanus*	50	Mar-May;F
PIKE, NORTHERN, *Esox lucius*	40/48/57	Mar-Apr-May
PUMPKINSEED, *Lepomis gibbosus*	68/ /82	May-Jun-Aug
QUILLBACK, *Carpiodes cyprinus*		Apr-May
REDHORSE, BLACK, *Moxostoma duquesnei*	55/ /73	Apr
REDHORSE, GOLDEN, *Moxostoma erythrurum*	59–60	May
REDHORSE, GREATER, *Moxostoma valenciennes*	61–66	May-Jul
REDHORSE, NORTHERN, *Moxostoma macrolepidotum*	52/ /72	Apr-Jun
REDHORSE, RIVER, *Moxostoma carinatum*	71–77	Spring
REDHORSE, SILVER, *Moxostoma anisurum*	55–56	Jun
SALMON, ATLANTIC, *Salmo salar*	40/ /60	Oct-Dec
SALMON, CHINOOK, *Oncorhynchus tshawytscha*	/57	Fall
SALMON, COHO, *Oncorhynchus kisutch*	/70	Fall-LWin
SALMON, LANDLOCKED, *Salmo salar*	45–55	Oct-Nov
SAUGER, *Stizostedion canadense*	39/ /55	May-Jun
SMELT, POND, *Hypomesus olidus*	40s	Apr-Jun
SPLAKE, *Salvelinus fontinalis × S. namaycush*		Oct-Nov
SQUAWFISH, NORTHERN, *Ptychocheilus oregonensis*	64	May-Jul
SQUAWFISH, SACREMENTO, *Ptylocheilus grandis*	57	Apr
STEELHEAD, *Salmo gairdneri*	50/ /60	Dec-Apr
STURGEON, LAKE, *Acipenser fulvescens*	53/55–64/66	Apr-Jun
STURGEON, SHOVELNOSE, *Scaphirhynchus platorhynchus*		Apr-Jul
SUCKER, LONGNOSE, *Catostomus catostomus*	41/	Apr-Jul
SUCKER, SPOTTED, *Minytrema melanops*	54/59–64/67	Mar-EJun
SUCKER, WHITE, *Catostomus commersoni*	50/	Mar-Jun
SUNFISH, GREEN, *Lepomis cyanellus*	68–82	May-Jun-Aug
SUNFISH, LONGEAR, *Lepomis megalotis*	74–77	Jun-Aug
SUNFISH, REDBREAST, *Enneacanthus auritis*	50/62–68/82	Jun
SUNFISH, REDEAR, *Lepomis microlophus*		Summer

Freshwater Sportfish	Temperature (Degrees F) Low/Peak/Hi	Season
SUNFISH, SPOTTED, *Lepomis punctatus*		May-Nov
TENCH, *Tinca tinca*		Jun-Jul
TROUT, BROOK, *Salvelinus fontinalis*	39/42/52	Sep-Nov
TROUT, BROWN, *Salmo trutta*	**44–48**	Nov-Jan
TROUT, CUTTHROAT, *Salmo clarki*	50/	Apr-Aug
TROUT, DOLLY VARDEN	(see DOLLY VARDEN)	
TROUT, GOLDEN, *Salmo aguabonita*	**44–50**	Jun-Jul
TROUT, LAKE, *Salvelinus namaycush*	45/51–55/59	Jun-Fall-Dec
TROUT, RAINBOW, *Salmo gairdneri*	40/50–55/60	Nov-Jul
WALLEYE, *Stizostedion vitreum*	37/44–48/61	Apr-Jun
WARMOUTH, *Lepomis gulosus*		May-Aug
WHITEFISH, ATLANTIC, *Coregonus sp*. [canadensis]		Oct-Dec
WHITEFISH, LAKE, *Coregonus clupeaformis*	33/42/46	Sep-Dec
WHITEFISH, MOUNTAIN, *Prosopium williamsoni*	**Below 42/54**	Sep-Feb
WHITEFISH, ROUND, *Prosopium cylindraceum*	**40–42/54**	Oct-Dec

Freshwater Baitfish	Temperature (Degrees F) Low/Peak/Hi	Season
CHUB, BLUEHEAD, *Hybopsis leptocephala*		Apr-Jul
CHUB, CREEK, *Semilotilus atromaculatus*	55/60–70	May-Jul
CHUB, FLATHEAD, *Hybopsis gracilis*		Jun-Aug
CHUB, HORNYHEAD, *Nocomis biguttatus*	65/ /82	May-Jun
CHUB, LAKE, *Couesius plumbeus*	**57–66**	Apr-Jun
CHUB, RIVER, *Hybopsis micropogon*	65/ /82	May-Aug
CHUB, SILVER, *Hybopsis streriana*	65/70+	May-Jun
CHUBSUCKERS, *Erimyzon spp*.		Spring
DACE, BLACKNOSE, *Rhinichthys atratulus*	60/70	May-Jun
DACE, FINESCALE, *Chrosomus neogaeus*		May-Jun
DACE, LONGNOSE, *Rhinichthys cataractae*	53/	May-Aug
DACE, PEARL, *Margariscus margarita*	**63–65**	Spring
DACE, NORTHERN REDBELLY, *Phoxinus eos*		May-Aug
DACE, SOUTHERN REDBELLY, *Phoxinus erythrogaster*		Spr-ESum

Freshwater Baitfish	Temperature (Degrees F) Low/Peak/Hi	Spawning Season
FALLFISH, *Semotilus corporatus*	62/	May-Jun
HOG SUCKER, NORTHERN, *Hypentelium nigricans*	60/	May/
KILLIFISH, BANDED, *Fundulus diaphanous*	70/74	May
KILLIFISHES, Cyprinodontidae		Spr-Sum
LOGPERCH, *Percina caprodes*		Jun
MADTOMS, *Noturus spp.*	**70s**	Spr-Sum
MINNOW, BLUNTNOSE, *Pimephales notatus*	68/	May-Aug
MINNOW, BRASSY, *Hybognathus hankinsoni*	**50–55**	May-Jun
MINNOW, CUTLIPS, *Exoglossum maxillingua*	**63–71**	May-Jul
MINNOW, FATHEAD, *Pimephales promelas*	60/**64**/66	Jun-Aug
MINNOW, MISSISSIPPI SILVERY, *Hybognathus nuchalis*	54/ /70	Apr-May
MINNOW, OZARK, *Notroopis nubilus*		LApr-EJul
MOSQUITOFISH, *Gambusia affinis*		May-Sep
MUDMINNOWS, *Umbra spp.*		Mar-May
SCULPIN, MOTTLED, *Cottus bairdi*	**50**	May-Jun
SCULPIN, SLIMY, *Cottus cognatus*	41/50s	May
SCULPINS, Cottidae		LWin-Sum
SHAD, GIZZARD, *Dorosoma cepedianum*	50/70–75/80	Apr-Jun
SHAD, THREADFIN, *Dorosoma petenense*	57/70	Spr-Fall
SHINER, BLACKCHIN, *Notropis heterodon*		May-Jun
SHINER, BLACKNOSE, *Notropis heterolepis*		Jul
SHINER, BLEEDING, *Notropis zonatus*		Apr-EJun
SHINER, BRIDLE, *Notropis bifrenatus*	57/ /81	May-Aug
SHINER, COMMON, *Notropis cornutus*	60/**65**/83	May-Jul
SHINER, EMERALD, *Notropis atherinoides*	**75**	Jun-Jul
SHINER, GOLDEN, *Notemigonus crysoleucas*	**68–70**	May-Aug
SHINER, REDFIN, *Notropis umbratilus*		Jul-Aug
SHINER, SPOTFIN, *Notropis spilopterus*		May-Aug
SHINER, SPOTTAIL, *Notropis hudsonius*	**68**	Jun-Jul
SILVERSIDE, BROOK, *Labidesthes sicculus*		**May-Jul**-Aug
STONECAT, *Notorus flavus*	**82**	**Jun-Aug**

Freshwater Baitfish	Temperature (Degrees F) Low/Peak/Hi	Season
STONEROLLER, *Campostoma anomalum*	54/ /81	Spring
SUCKER, MOUNTAIN, *Catostomus platyrhynchus*	51/ /66	Jun-Aug
TOPMINNOWS, *Fundulus spp*.		Spr-Sum
TROUT-PERCH, *Percopsis omiscomaycus*	43/61–68	May-Aug

Anadromous & Brackish-Spawning Fishes	Temperature (Degrees F) Low/Peak/Hi	Season
ALEWIFE, *Alosa pseudoharengus*	51/**55–72**/81	Mar-Aug
ANCHOVY, BAY, *Anchoa mitchilli*	68/	Apr-Nov
BASS, STRIPED, *Morone saxatilis*	55/**60–67**/70	Feb-Jul
CATFISH, HARDHEAD, *Arius felis*	55/**60–65**/75	May-Aug
CHAR, ARCTIC, *Salvelinus alpinus*	**Below 40**	Sep-Mar
CISCO, ARCTIC, *Coregonus autumnalis*		Jul-Aug
DOLLY VARDEN, *Salvelinus malma*	42/**44–46**	Sep-Nov
EULACHON, *Thaleichthys pacificus*	**40–46**	Mar-May
GOOSEFISH, *Lophius americanus*		May-Aug
HERRING, BLUEBACK, *Alosa aestivalis*	57/70/81	Apr-Jun
HERRING, SKIPJACK, *Alosa chrysochloris*		May-Jul
KILLIFISH, STRIPED, *Fundulus majalis*		Apr-Sep
MINNOW, SHEEPSHEAD, *Cyprinodon variegatus*		Apr-LSum
MUMMICHOG, *Fundulus heteroclitus*		Jun-Jul
PERCH, SILVER, *Bairdiella chrysoura*		LSpr-Sum
PERCH, WHITE, *Morone americana*	50/**57–61**/66	Mar-**Jun**-Jul
SALMON, CHINOOK, *Oncorhynchus tshawytscha*	**42–57**/70	Aug-Nov
SALMON, CHUM, *Oncorhynchus keta*	50/53/57	Jul-**LFall**-Dec
SALMON, COHO, *Oncorhynchus kisutch*	/70	**Oct**-Mar
SALMON, PINK, *Oncorhynchus gorbuscha*	**50/61**	Jul-Oct
SALMON, SOCKEYE, *Oncorhynchus nerka*	37/**43–45**/55	Jul-Dec
SHAD, ALABAMA, *Alosa alabamae*	**66–69**/72	Jun-Jul
SHAD, AMERICAN, *Alosa sapidissima*	54/**62–67**	Jan-Jul Apr-Oct, Calif
SHAD, HICKORY, *Alosa mediocris*	**50–52**/	May-Jun
SILVERSIDE, ATLANTIC, *Menidia menidia*	55/**61** + /86	LMar-Jul
SMELT, NIGHT, *Spirinchus starksi*		Jan-Sep
SMELT, RAINBOW, *Osmerus mordax*	36/**50–59**/65	Mar-May
SMELT, SURF, *Hypomesus pretiosus*		**Jun-Sep**;YR
SNOOK, *Centropomus undecimalis*		May-Nov
STEELHEAD, *Salmo gairdneri*		Nov-**Spr**-Aug

Anadromous & Brackish-Spawning Fishes	Temperature (Degrees F) Low/Peak/Hi	Season
STURGEON, ATLANTIC, *Acipenser oxyrhynchus*	56–64	Feb-EJul
STURGEON, GREEN, *Acipenser medirostris*		May-Jul
STURGEON, SHORTNOSE, *Acipenser brevirostrum*		Apr-EJun
STURGEON, WHITE, *Acipenser transmontanus*	48/62/75	May-Jun
TARPON, *Megalops atlanticus*		May-Sep
TOMCOD, ATLANTIC, *Microgadus tomcod*	32/ /39	Nov-Feb
TROUT, COASTAL CUTTHROAT, *Salmo clarki*	45/50s	Jan-**Spr**

Saltwater Fishes	Season
ALBACORE, *Thunnus alalunga*	LSum-Fall
ANCHOVY, NORTHERN, *Engraulis mordax*	YR; **Win-Spr**
BARRACUDA, PACIFIC, *Sphyraena spp.*	Apr-**May-Jun**-Sep
BASS, BLACK SEA, *Centropristis striata*	Mar-Apr;Jun-Aug
BASS, GIANT SEA, *Stereolepis gigas*	Jun-**Jul-Sep**
BASS, KELP, *Paralabrax clathratus*	May-**Jul**-Aug
BLUEFISH, *Pomatomus saltatrix*	Apr-May;Jun-Aug
BOCACCIO, *Sebastes paucispinis*	**Dec-Apr**
BONITO, PACIFIC, *Sarda chiliensis*	**LJan-May**
CABEZON, *Scorpaenichthys marmoratus*	Nov-**Jan**-May
COD, ATLANTIC, *Gadus morhua*	Jan-Mar
CORBINA, CALIFORNIA, *Menticirrhus undulatus*	June-**Jul-Aug**-Sep
CROAKER, ATLANTIC, *Micropogon undulatus*	Sep-Mar
CROAKER, SPOTFIN, *Roncador stearnsi*	Jun-Sep
CROAKER, WHITE, *Genyonemus lineatus*	YR;**ESpr**
DOGFISH, SMOOTH, *Mustelus canis*	May-Jul
DOGFISH, SPINY, *Squalus acanthias*	Nov-Mar
DRUM, RED, *Sciaenops ocellatus*	Apr-Sep
FLOUNDER, SOUTHERN, *Paralichthys lethostigma*	Sep-Feb
FLOUNDER, STARRY, *Platichthys stellatus*	Nov-**Dec-Jan**-Feb
FLOUNDER, SUMMER, *Paralichthys dentatus*	Sep-Feb
FLOUNDER YELLOWTAIL, *Limanda ferruginea*	Apr-May
FLYINGFISHES, Exocoetidae	May-Aug
GOOSEFISH, *Lophius americanus*	May-Aug
GREENLING, KELP, *Hexagrammos decagrammus*	**Oct-Nov**-Win
GUITARFISH, SHOVELNOSE, *Rhinobatos productus*	Spr-Sum
HADDOCK, *Melanogrammus aeglefinus*	Apr-Jun
HAKE, RED, *Urophycis chuss*	Jul-Aug

Saltwater Fishes	Season
HAKE, SILVER, *Merluccius bilinearis*	Jun-Aug
HAKE, WHITE, *Urophycis tenuis*	Summer
HALFMOON, *Medialuna californiensis*	Sum-Fall
HALIBUT, CALIFORNIA, *Paralichythys californicus*	Apr-Jul
HERRING, ATLANTIC, *Clupea harengus harengus*	Sep-Oct
JACK MACKEREL, *Trachurus symmetricus*	**Mar-Jul**
JACKSMELT, *Atherinops californiensis*	Oct-Mar
LINGCOD, *Ophidion elongatus*	Dec-Mar
MACKEREL, ATLANTIC, *Scomber scombrus*	Apr-Jun
MACKEREL, CHUB, *Scomber japonicus*	**Mar-May**, Calif.
MENHADEN, ATLANTIC, *Brevoortia tyrannus*	**Jun-Aug**
MUDSUCKER, LONGJAW, *Gillichthys mirabilis*	Jan-Jul
OPALEYE, *Girella nigricans*	LSpr-Sum
PERCH, BLACK, *Embiotoca jacksoni*	YR; **Spr-Sum**
PERCH, SHINER, *Cymatogaster aggregata*	Spr-Sum
PORGY, RED, *Pargus sedecim*	May-Aug
PRICKLEBACK, MONKEYFACE, *Cebidichthys violaceous*	Mar-EMay
QUEENFISH, *Seriphus politus*	May-Oct
ROCKFISH, BLUE, *Sebastes mysticinus*	Nov-Mar
ROCKFISH, GRASS, *Sebastes rastrelliger*	Mar-Sep
ROCKFISH, KELP, *Sebastes atrovirens*	Apr-Aug
ROCKFISH, OLIVE, *Sebastes serranoides*	Dec-Mar
ROCKFISH, VERMILION, *Sebastes miniatus*	Dec-Mar
SANDDAB, LONGFIN, *Citharichthys xanthostigma*	**Jul-Sep**
SANDDAB, PACIFIC, *Citharichthys sordidus*	**Jul-Sep**
SARGO, *Anisotremus davidsoni*	LSpr-ESum
SCORPIONFISH, CALIFORNIA, *Scorpaena guttata*	Apr-Aug
SCUP, *Stenotomus chrysops*	May-Aug
SEABASS, WHITE, *Atractoscion nobilis*	LSpr-Sum
SHEEPHEAD, CALIFORNIA, *Pimelometopon pulchrum*	**Sum**
SMELT, DELTA, *Hypomesus transpacificus*	LWin-ESpr
SMELT, NIGHT, *Spirinchus starksi*	Mar-Fall
SMELT, SURF, *Hypomesus pretiosus*	Mar-Fall
SURFPERCH, BARRED, *Amphisticus argenteus*	Mar-Jul
SURFPERCH, WALLEYE, *Hyperprosopon argenteum*	Spring
TURBOT, DIAMOND, *Hypsopsetta guttulata*	ESpr
WHITEFISH, OCEAN, *Caulolatilus princeps*	Fall-ESpr
YELLOWTAIL, CALIFORNIA, *Seriola lalandei dorsalis*	Jun-**Jul-Aug**-Sep

FISH-HANDLING HAZARDS

Some of the fish we catch must be handled with care because of sharp teeth, spines, scales, gill covers, and other body parts. Some are even dangerous, because of their size, the sharpness of their sharp parts, or the toxicity of spines. Even those fish that do not inject toxins when they bite or stab can cause serious infections. Because the dangerous parts vary from fish to fish, it is good to handle all fish with care and to handle some of them with extreme care. Any large fish—no matter how lacking in armament—can be very dangerous once it starts thrashing around with its big, muscular body and tail.

Venomous Fish

Numerous fish species are capable of delivering a dose of venom along with a jab. Such venoms are known as ichthyocanthotoxins, Latin for "fish spine poisons." Toxicity varies from species to species, and the most venomous fish in the world is the stonefish, fortunately not found in North American waters, but restricted to the Indian and western Pacific oceans. However, the lionfish (also known as zebrafish and turkey fish) and several other of the scorpionfishes are also quite venomous and must be handled with extreme care. Venomous spines may be located almost anywhere: dorsal fins, pectoral fins, anal fins, pelvic fins, tails. Since many of these venomous fishes are edible, care must be taken not only in handling, but also in seeing that these spines and the venom glands to which they are attached are removed without contaminating the flesh.

Venomous species in our waters include:

> Catfishes (Siluroidei)
> Horn Sharks (Heterodontidae)
> Rabbitfish (Siganidae)
> Scorpionfishes (Scorpaenidae)
> Spiny Dogfishes (Squalidae)
> Stargazers (Uranoscopidae)
> Stingrays and other spined rays (Rajiiformes)
> Surgeonfishes (Acanthuridae)
> Toadfishes (Batrachoidae)

Symptoms vary with the species and the amount of venom received, but may include stinging, burning, throbbing to intense pain, redness and swelling, numbness, tissue sloughing, falling blood pressure, rapid pulse, vomiting, diarrhea, fever, sweating, muscular paralysis, delirium, death.

First-aid treatment should begin immediately. Flush the wound with clean water or urine (it's actually almost sterile). Allow the wound to bleed; it may be necessary to apply suction to a puncture wound. Soak the wound in **hot** water or apply very hot compresses (as hot as the person can stand) for thirty to sixty minutes. Cover the wound with antiseptic and sterile dressing. Get medical care.

Other Venomous Species

While fishing, the angler may encounter venomous species other than fish.

Jellyfish, Sea Nettles, Portuguese Men-of-war, Sea Wasps, Hydroids, and **Sea Anemones** are familiar to most saltwater anglers, but the newcomer to sea or estuary fishing may not be able to recognize the stinging species or know what to do when stung. In general, avoid those with tentacles and handle all of them with gloves, other tools, and care. Symptoms are almost immediate and obvious, and vary in severity from the slight irritation of the few venomous anemones to the sting of the tropical Pacific sea wasp or box jellyfish, which can cause death in seconds or minutes. For most of these stings, however, first-aid treatment is sufficient. First, remove the tentacles gently so that additional venom is not injected (do not rub), perhaps followed by shaving the area with a razor or sharp knife. Do not apply water or anything acidic. Instead, use an alkaline solution such as ammonia, sodium bicarbonate, urine, alum, alcohol, high-proof liquor, or other liquid with a high alcohol content. This can be followed by the application of papaya juice or meat tenderizer. In severe cases, treatment for shock or respiratory distress may be necessary.

Fire Corals and Fire Sponges, found in subtropical oceans, cause reactions similar to those caused by jellyfish, and treatment is the same.

Sea Snakes occur only in the Indian and Pacific oceans and are not very aggressive. Some are actually downright docile. However, they are more than ten times more venomous than any other snake. Fortunately, their mouths are small and their fangs are very short and located in the rear of the mouth, so they have to chew the venom in. In the majority of bite cases, no serious envenomation results. The first noticeable symptom, paralysis, doesn't usually show up for several hours. The mortality rate is about 17 percent, and death may occur a week or more after the bite. Antivenin is available and should be administrated as soon as possible. In the meantime, first-aid treatment involves complete immobilization of the victim and the use of a restricting band. Neurotoxin absorption is too rapid for cutting and suction to do much good.

Generally Hazardous Fish

Obviously, many fish have sharp teeth and can bite. And many have sharp, strong spines that can deliver painful puncture wounds. Even if the spines aren't venomous, complications can result from mucus, slime, and bacteria in the puncture wound. Still others have electrical organs that can shock, skin that can scratch or irritate, sharp-edged gill covers and fins. Most fishermen learn rather quickly how to handle these hazards, but the big danger comes when you catch a fish you aren't familiar with. When in doubt, try to avoid touching the fish with the bare hands, stay clear of mouth and fins, and use a landing net or gaff (a lip gaff, if you plan to release your catch) to lift the fish, rather than lifting it by its gill covers, mouth, or caudal peduncle (the thin part of the body just forward of the tail). This list isn't complete, but it may help you avoid trouble:

Agujon: Sharp bill
Barbfish: Venomous dorsal, anal, and pelvic fin spines
Barracudas: Sharp teeth
Billfish: Sharp bill; sharp keels on caudal peduncle; sharp edges on caudal (tail) fin
Bass, Black: First dorsal and anal fin spines
Bass, Kelp: Dorsal fin spines; spines on head and gill covers
Bass, Sea: Dorsal fin spines; spines on head and gill covers
Bass, Striped: First dorsal and anal fin spines
Bass, White and Yellow: First dorsal and anal fin spines
Bluefish: Extremely sharp teeth
Bluegill: Dorsal fin spines
Boxfish: Toxic skin slime (especially irritating to eyes)
Bullheads: Dorsal and pectoral fin spines
Catfish: Dorsal and pectoral fin spines (venomous in 47 species worldwide)
Cod: Abrasive gill rakers
Conger Eels: Teeth
Cowfish: Toxic skin slime (especially irritating to eyes)

Croaker: Gill-cover spines

Cunner: Dorsal and anal fin spines; teeth

Dogfish, Spiny: Dorsal fin spine (mildly venomous)

Filefish: Toxic skin slime (especially irritating to eyes)

Flounder, Summer (Fluke): Sharp teeth

Gars: Teeth

Goosefish: Teeth; dorsal fin spines

Groupers: Sharp fin spines and gill rakers; barbed gill covers

Grunts: Dorsal and anal fin spines

Gurnards: Fin spines; spines on heads and gill covers

Hagfish: Toxic skin slime (especially irritating to eyes)

Halibut, Atlantic: Sharp caudal peduncle and base of caudal (tail) fin

Halibut, California: Sharp teeth

Houndfish: Sharp bill

Lampreys: Toxic skin slime (especially irritating to eyes)

Lionfish: Venomous dorsal, anal, and pelvic fin spines

Mantas: Wings and tails

Marlin: Sharp bill

Morays: Sharp teeth; toxic skin slime (especially irritating to eyes)

Muskellunge: Teeth

Needlefish: Sharp bill

Octopus: Beak

Perch, Ocean (Rosefish): Dorsal fin spines; spines on head and gill covers

Perch, Yellow and White: First dorsal fin spines

Pickerel: Teeth

Pike: Teeth

Porcupinefish: Body spines; toxic skin slime (especially irritating to eyes)

Porgies: Dorsal and anal fin spines

Puffers: Toxic skin slime (especially irritating to eyes)

Rabbitfish: Venomous fin spines (8 species)

Rays, Bat: Venomous tail spines

Rays, Electric: Electrical shock; tail spines

Rockfish (Rock Cods): Dorsal fin spines; spines on head and gill covers

Sailfish: Sharp bill; sharp edges of caudal (tail) fin and caudal peduncle keels

Sauger: Teeth; fin spines; sharp gill cover edges; rough, sharp scales on big ones

Scorpionfish: Venomous dorsal, anal, and pelvic fin spines (57 species)

Sculpins: Fin spines; spines on body, head and gill covers

Scup (Porgy): Fin spines

Searobins: Fin spines; spines on head and gill covers

Seatrout: Teeth; front dorsal fin spines

Sharks: Teeth; abrasive dermal denticles (scales) of some

Sharks, Horn: Venomous dorsal fin spines

Sheepshead: Teeth; dorsal and anal fin spines

Skates: Rough skin, sharp spines on body (some species)

Snapper, Cubera: Large sharp teeth

Snappers: Sharp teeth; pointed gill covers

Snook: Sharp-edged gill covers

Soapfish: Toxic skin slime (especially irritating to eyes)

Spearfish: Sharp bill

Squid: Slime on hands can cause disease

Stargazers: Sharp spine on dorsal fin (venomous in 3 species); electrical shock

Stingrays: Venomous spine on tail and/or back (58 species worldwide)

Sunfish: Dorsal fin spines

Surgeonfish: Sharp spines on caudal peduncle

Swordfish: Sharp bill

Tangs: Sharp spines on caudal peduncle

Tarpon: Sharp scales

Tautog: Dorsal and anal fin spines; teeth

Tilefish: Barbed gill covers

Toadfish: Teeth; venomous body and fin spines; toxic skin slime (especially irritating to eyes)

Torpedos (Torpedo Rays): Electrical shock

Triggerfish: Erectile spine ahead of dorsal fin

Trunkfish: Toxic skin slime (especially irritating to eyes)

Walleye: Teeth; fin spines; sharp-edged gill covers; rough, sharp scales on big ones

Weakfish: Teeth; front dorsal fin spines

Weeverfish: Venomous spines (4 species)

Wolffish: Teeth

Zebrafish: Venomous spines in all fins

HOW TO CALCULATE A FISH'S WEIGHT WITHOUT A SCALE

The best way to calculate a fish's weight is to use an accurate scale. That's obvious. But what do you do when you left your scale in another tackle box, or the fish in question is too heavy (or, alas, too light) for your scale? All is not lost, and of the several methods that have been devised for estimating a fish's weight without a scale, here are three.

THE GIRTH-SQUARED METHOD

This method of weight calculation is not accurate enough for record applications, but it is close enough for most purposes. It works best on fish with "normal" or cylindrical shapes, and won't be very useful on flounders and other flatfish or on fish that are flattened vertically, like spadefish. Here is the formula:

$$W = L \times G^2 / K$$

W = Weight in pounds
L = Length in inches
G = Girth in inches (squared)
K = 800 for fish with "normal" shapes (bass, trout, etc.); 900 for long, cylindrical fish (pike, gar, barracuda, etc.)

Example: If you catch a rainbow trout that is 14 inches long and has a girth of 16 inches, you would estimate its weight by multiplying its length times the square of its girth, then dividing by 800:

$$14 \times 16 \times 16 = 3584 / 800 = 4.48$$

Congratulations! You've just caught a fat, 4½-pound trout.

STURDY'S SCALE FOR SALMON

Back in 1893 an English angler named Sturdy published an estimated-weight scale for salmon which was in use for many years. In fact, for a while it was used to estimate the weights of many other fish as well. Obviously, any scale based solely on a relationship between length and weight cannot be as accurate as the previous method, which at least takes girth into account. However, if you are catching and releasing salmon (or very large trout), you may not want to mess around with girth measurements. So, if your salmon (or other fish of "normal" shape and density) is in average condition, the following scale may be accurate enough to revive.

Length in.	Weight lb.
30	11½
31	12¾
32	14
33	15½
34	16¾
35	18¼
36	20
37	21¾
38	23½
39	25¼
40	27½
41	29½
42	31¾
43	34
44	36½
45	39
46	41¾
47	44½
48	47½
49	50½
50	53½

MONA'S SCALE FOR PIKE

Here is another British method of estimating weight from length, this time for pike. It should work as well on big pickerel, and perhaps its ballpark accuracy might even serve for muskies and barracudas. (The original scale gave weight to three decimal places, but I figured that was a bit too precise for a scale that is only a rough estimate.)

None of these methods is truly accurate, but they are good enough for spinning winter yarns before the fireplace. And all are a lot better than killing fish just to weigh them. If we keep doing that sort of thing, all our bragging stories will be about the long-gone "good old days."

Length in.	Weight lb.	Length in.	Weight lb.
20	2.5	40	20.0
21	2.9	41	21.5
22	3.3	42	23.2
23	3.8	43	24.8
24	4.3	44	26.6
25	4.9	45	28.5
26	5.5	46	30.5
27	6.2	47	32.4
28	6.9	48	34.6
29	7.6	49	36.8
30	8.4	50	39.1
31	9.3	51	41.5
32	10.2	52	43.9
33	11.2	53	46.5
34	12.3	54	49.2
35	13.4	55	52.0
36	14.6	56	54.9
37	15.8	57	57.9
38	17.1	58	61.0
39	18.5	59	64.2
		60	67.5

FISHING

FLY-FISHING

In fly-fishing, presentation is everything. Distance, delicacy, accuracy, speed, power—they're all part of the casting presentation. In spinning, spincasting, or baitcasting, the weighted lure or sinker is what's being cast, and it drags the leader and line behind it through the air. In fly-fishing, it is the weight of the line that's being cast, so the balance or relationship of line, leader, and fly is crucial to fly-casting success.

The specifications and properties of fly lines and leader materials are discussed in the Tackle section that follows this one, but we are concerned with balancing them here. The size or weight of the fly line determines what rod can be used to cast it, and line weight also affects the power and delicacy of the presentation. Because tippets are the weakest links in the fly-fisherman's armament, tippet size is perhaps the next most important variable. Finally, matching the hatch requires that a fly of a given size and wind resistance be selected. So, balancing fly tackle usually requires a certain amount of juggling and compromise.

Preassembled fly leaders and fly tippet materials are identified by an X size number, although the heavier tippets use a /5 numbering system. From brand to brand, there may be a considerable difference in the breaking strength of the tippet material in any given size, but the diameter of the material ought to be approximately the same.

This difference in breaking strength within a given diameter or size will be accompanied by a corresponding difference in stiffness. Generally, the stronger the material is, the stiffer it will be. Small dry flies and nymphs need limp tippets, so they can have maximum freedom of movement. Larger dry flies, wet flies, and streamers need stiffer tippets, because they will turn the fly over better at the end of a cast. Bass bugs and wind-resistant saltwater flies require the stiffest tippets.

BALANCING FLY SIZE TO TIPPET

In all fishing, it is important that each part of your equipment be in balance with every other part. This is particularly important when it comes to matching flies, especially dry flies, and tippets. In the chart that follows, a fairly wide range of fly sizes is presented for each tippet size, with considerable overlap. Streamers, bass bugs, saltwater flies, and the bulkier wet flies and terrestrials can take somewhat larger tippets than dry flies, nymphs, skimpy terrestrials, and most wet flies. Whether you can afford to tie on flies of all sizes within the range listed depends upon fishing conditions. The clearer and stiller the water, the brighter and hotter the day, the warier the fish, the more you should opt for the smallest tippet recommended for the flies you have chosen to fish. If the sky is overcast, the wind is blowing, the water is murky and flowing fast, and the fish are feeding aggressively, you can go with the larger tippets listed.

Tippet Size	Fly Size
6/5 .015 in.	6/0–3/0
7/5 .014	5/0–2/0
8/5 .013	3/0–2
9/5 .012	2/0–2
0X .011	1/0–2
1X .010	2–8
2X .009	6–10
3X .008	6–14
4X .007	6–16
5X .006	8–18
6X .005	10–22
7X .004	14–26
8X .003	18–32

The Rule of 4 for Balancing Fly and Tippet Sizes

This rule, which should be viewed as a guideline rather than a rigid prescription, is very simple:

> **Divide the hook size by 4 to determine**
> **the proper X size of the tippet.**

But don't forget to take the tippet material's stiffness into account.

PUTTING IT ALL TOGETHER:
FLY LINE, LEADER, TIPPET AND FLY

Most fly leaders are tapered—graduated in size from the thick butt end that is attached to the fly line down to the delicate tippet that is attached to the fly—so the balancing act requires that you take several factors into account.

With years of experience, you will develop your own methods and formulas, but for relative newcomers to fly-fishing, like me, here is a table from 3M/Scientific Anglers that can help sort out the balancing act:

Line Weight	Butt Diameter	Tippet Size	Fly Size
3–4	.017 in.	4X–8X	14–28
5	.019	3X–7X	12–22 (dries); to size 4 (streamers)
6–7	.021	0X–5X	To size 8 (dries); to size 5 (streamers)
8–9	.023	2X or larger	4–3/0
10–15	.025	0X or larger	2–4/0

As you can see from the table, the bulkiness or air-resistance of the fly makes a difference in the appropriate size. Other variables must also be taken into account. One is the relative stiffness of the leader material, particularly the tippet material, which will affect tippet strength. The others are the taper and buoyancy of the fly line itself.

If you are casting a weight-forward, bass-bug taper, or saltwater taper line, it will not cast the same as a double-taper line of the same weight, unless you have thirty feet of line in the air during the backcast. (As you will see in the Tackle section, the weight of the forwardmost thirty feet of a fly line determines its size rating.) Some (but by no means all) fly-casting experts recommend that you consider such a line the equivalent of the next larger size double-taper fly line. In other words, they say, a WF5 line will cast more nearly like a DT6 than a DT5. I haven't yet gained enough control over my fly-casting to tell whether the taper makes that much difference. But I can tell you for sure that the line's buoyancy or function does. A sinking or sink-tip line casts very differently from a floating line. If I like the way a rod handles a DT6F line, I *know* I won't like the way it casts a WF6S or WF6F/S. In such cases, I prefer to drop down to a 5-weight sinking or sink-tip line.

WATER TEMPERATURE AND SALMON FLIES

Atlantic salmon are notoriously finicky, unpredictable creatures, and catching one isn't easy. When in fresh water, it is generally, but not universally believed, salmon don't feed at all. Yet they can, at times, be induced to take flies, spoons, spinners, plugs, even natural baits. Whether they strike (or "take," as many salmon fishermen insist) out of instinct, aggression, defense, or curiosity is anyone's guess. At any rate, while matching the hatch is not part of fly-fishing for salmon, proper fly selection is. Color, pattern, and size of fly do seem to make a difference at times, and some British salmon fishers have discerned a definite correlation between water temperature and fly size: The warmer the temperature, the smaller the fly.

Water Temperature		Fly Size
9°C	48–49°F	4
10	50–51	5
11	52–53	6
12	54–55	7
13–14	56–57	8
15	58–59	9
16 and up	60 and up	10, 12, 14

These size recommendations apply to flies fished on a floating fly line in relatively low water. In higher, colder water, many salmon fishermen opt for sinking or sink-tip lines (or spinning outfits), and fly size isn't so easily correlated to water temperature then. However, fly *type* is.

In salmon rivers, water temperature and water depth often are directly related to each other (high waters being colder than low summer waters), so no one is quite sure whether the relationship of fly type to water is more closely tied to temperature or depth. Those who fish by the thermometer may find these relationships useful:

Water Temperature	Fly Type
Below 48°F (9°C)	Sinking Wet Flies, Tube Flies, Streamers (often fished on sinking or sink-tip lines)
50–60°F (10–15°C)	Wet Flies (fished near top on floating lines)
Over 60°F (15.6°C)	Dry Flies
Over 65°F (18°C)	Spoons, Spinners, Natural Baits (trolled fairly deep in lakes for landlocked salmon). Probably too warm for fly-fishing anadromous salmon

MATCHING THE HATCH

Devout hatch-matchers say that when busily feeding trout (and other fish) ignore your fly, it is because your ersatz offering imitates the wrong species of insect. I am dubious that a fish will mistake your tied fly for the real thing, yet be able to tell that it imitates the wrong species. (Consider that the Light Cahill fly can be used to imitate at least these eight different flies: *Cinygma dimicki, Epeorus vitreus, Heptagenia elegantula, Stenacron interpunctatum,* and *Stenonema ithaca, S. luteum, S. femoratum,* and *S. modestum.*) If your bogus bug is in the right ballpark in terms of size and shade, it is far more likely that your faulty presentation technique is responsible for your failure.

There are those who carry streamside tying kits so they can match whatever is hatching. Others, a larger number, just carry little nets so they can capture and study the bugs at close hand, the better to select a lookalike from their fly boxes. Either approach is fine for those who need a secondary hobby, but, as the bumper sticker says, I'd rather be fishing.

My personal approach to matching the hatch—admittedly a casual and perhaps even primitive one—is borrowed from other forms of fishing. If I determine (and sometimes I'm just guessing) that fish are feeding on a given prey—whether it's an insect, a forage fish, or a bottom-dwelling crustacean—I will try to approximate the natural prey when I select a fly. That means I'll try to come close to it in size, shape, and color. (More important, I'll try to put it where the fish are feeding: on the surface, down on the bottom, or somewhere in between.) Most of the time, close is close enough.

But sometimes it isn't. If my first guess doesn't take fish, I'll guess again. And I'll keep guessing until I find something that works—all the while watching what's happening in and around the stream. Every clue helps. Sometimes it will be fairly obvious what fish are feeding on—a little, cream-colored mayfly in about size 16, say—yet nothing in your box that looks right will attract a strike. In such cases I will sometimes resort to a fly of a different size, shape, and color altogether, and sometimes even a different type. If I'm really frustrated, or just have a desperate need to eat a trout, I might even depart from orthodoxy altogether and tie on a plastic Bingo Bug or Frisky Fly. They usually succeed in catching fish, as well as infuriating purists. But most of the time I can find a more conventional fly, nymph, or streamer that will work. Too often I have borrowed the "right" fly from a friendly hatch-matcher and still failed to score against finicky fish, thanks to my faulty technique.

Matching the hatch works, and at times it's important, perhaps even crucial, to successful angling. But don't let its mysteries deter you from using a fly rod, especially for trout. (Trout are so much more fun to catch on a fly rod. I have given up fishing for them any other way, even though I can usually catch more of them with spinning gear.) You needn't become a fly-tier or entomologist to succeed at fly-fishing. Anxiety and self-doubt ruin more fly-rod outings than do any real or imagined inadequacies in insect identification. In fly-fishing, as in all other forms of angling, you simply must know your fish, be alert to what's going on around you, and use your angling wits to fool a fish into feeding upon, attacking, testing, worrying, or otherwise biting your hook. Matching the hatch is just another angling tool.

ENTOMOLOGICAL GLOSSARY FOR FLY-FISHERMEN

Unfortunately, a little entomological terminology is in order before we can get down to the brass tacks of matching the hatch.

Abdomen: That portion of an insect's body located between the thorax (legged portion) and tail; various filaments, hairs, and platelike or filamentous gills may be attached to the abdominal segments, but not legs. [See also **Body.**]

Attractor fly: A fly that does not imitate a specific insect, but that attracts a fish for reasons other than its matching the hatch (such as Royal Coachman, Humpies, Wulffs, Bivisibles, and the like).

Bass bug: A fairly bulky floating artificial lure used in fly-rodding for bass, panfish, and certain other fish, including large trout. May be an attractor pattern, or may imitate a dragonfly, damselfly, grasshopper, other large aquatic or terrestrial insect, mouse, frog, salamander, or the like.

Body: Insect's thorax and abdomen, collectively; as used by fly-tiers, refers principally to the abdomen, the thorax's appearance being suggested by the hackle.

Caddisflies: Aquatic insects of the order Trichoptera.

Damselflies: Aquatic insects of the suborder Zygoptera (order Odonata), whose wings are usually held above the body at rest; larval forms (nymphs) frequently used for trout, bass, sunfish.

Downwings: Collective term for caddisflies, stoneflies, and midges.

Dragonflies: Aquatic insects of the order Odonata (and sometimes particularly of the suborder Anisoptera, whose wings are outspread laterally from the body when at rest); larvae have provided numerous important nymph patterns.

Dry fly: Floating insect imitation, often of the adult (imago) form; in mayfly imitations, may be tied as a dun or spinner.

Dun: The subimago (subadult) emergent mayfly form during metamorphosis.

Flatwings: Stoneflies.

Half-spent: Descriptive of late adult stage, during or immediately after deposition of eggs.

Imago: Sexually mature, adult stage of insect following metamorphosis.

Midges: Tiny aquatic insects belonging to the family Chironomidae (although flies imitating other members of the order Diptera are sometimes also called midges).

Mayflies: Aquatic insects of the order Ephemeroptera, which account for most of the important hatches; tied and fished as nymphs, duns, and spinners.

Nymph: (1) The larval, pupal, or nymphal stage early in an insect's development; (2) a wingless, sinking fly tied to imitate it or other wingless aquatic creatures, for instance, scuds.

Pupa: Development stage immediately preceding adult stages in insects with complete metamorphosis.

Scuds: Any of several freshwater crustaceans of the order Amphipoda, which are important fish foods and have supplied numerous nymph patterns.

Sowbugs: Freshwater crustaceans of the order Isopoda, sometimes used to pattern flies for nymph fishing.

Spent: Descriptive of late adult stage, after eggs have been deposited.

Spinner: Adult or imago stage in mayfly development.

Stoneflies: Aquatic insects of the order Plecoptera, tied and fished as nymphs and wet and dry flies.

Subimago: Winged, subadult (dun) stage in mayfly development.

Tentwings: Caddisflies.

Terrestrial: Short for "terrestrial insect"; fly tied to imitate a terrestrial or nonaquatic insect, such as ant, bee, beetle, cricket, grasshopper, and so on.

Thorax: Portion of an insect's body between the head and abdomen; the six legs are attached to the thorax.

Trico: Abbreviated form of *Trichorythodes,* an important genus of small mayflies often called tiny whitewinged blacks.

Upwings: Mayflies.

Water bugs: Aquatic insects belonging to the order Hemiptera, including backswimmers, water boatmen, water striders, and the like; wet flies imitating them are of local or limited angling importance.

Wet fly: Imitation insect tied so that it will sink in the water; may imitate nymphal, preemergent, or spent adult form.

MAJOR HATCHES

Really dedicated hatch-matchers are probably eligible for master's degrees in entomology, but the average fly-fisherman needn't get that deeply involved. Still, you must begin somewhere, if only to have a box stocked with flies that will at least come close to matching the really important hatches you may encounter. I love looking at and buying fishing tackle, so I own and carry more flies than most beginners really need. You can probably get by with a selection of dries, wets, nymphs, and streamers in assorted sizes and light, medium, and dark shades. But there are some truly important hatches it may be worth matching even more closely.

Students of streamside entomology tell me that hatches are fairly dependable in terms of their chronological order. Sometimes their appearance is quite predictable even as to calendar date and time of day. (Doug Swisher and Carl Richards have espoused a theory that insects will hatch during the most pleasant time of day. Early and late in the season, that means midmorning to midafternoon; in the heat of summer, early in the morning or toward nightfall. It makes sense.)

Angling author and book publisher Nick Lyons and editor Tom Rosenbauer of *The Orvis News* suggest a list of the most important hatches on trout streams around the country. My treatment of their suggestions follows. I don't think you have to know the names of the emerging insects to imitate them (I never can remember their names), but I have supplied the scientific names for those who want to practice their Latin or converse with really serious fly-fishermen. More important, the Latin names are necessary to be certain we are all talking about the same bug.

In the case of adult mayflies (spinners), wing color can be assumed to be hyaline (translucent or nearly transparent) unless otherwise specified.

Coast to Coast Hatches

Tricos/Tiny Whitewinged Blacks, *Tricorythodes spp.:* 3–6 mm (20–28 hook); nymph, dark brown (sometimes w/ light rings on abdomen); dun, pale olive gray to brownish black body, whitish or pale creamy wings; spinner, creamy brown to brownish black; June through September; usually morning emergence, morning to midday spinner fall; quiet to medium-speed water w/ silt and debris; also called Tiny Whitewinged Trico, Black Hen Spinner, Reverse Jenny Spinner, Dark Brown Spinner, Pale Olive Dun; Snowflake or Snowflake Mayfly (esp. *T. explicatus, T. stygiatus, T. attratus*); Tiny Whitewinged Black Quill *(T. stygiatus, T. attratus);* Tiny Whitewinged Brown Quill *(T. allectus);* Tiny Whitewinged Claret Quill *(T. minutus, T. fallax)*

Caddisflies, Order Trichoptera: Numerous species in more than a dozen families of various forms, sizes, and colors, which appear at various times throughout the season; among the best-known caddis patterns, especially nymph, wet, and drowned patterns, are White Miller, Grizzly King, Yellow Caddis Worm, Orange Caddis Worm, Little Black Caddis, Spotted Sedge, Little Western Sedge, Small Spotted Sedge, Green Caddis, Grannom and American Grannom, Dark Gray Caddis, Dark Brown Caddis, Shadfly, American Sedge, Autumn Phantom, Orange Sedge, Giant Red Sedge, Dark Blue Sedge, Medium Brown Sedge, Pale Microcaddis Pupa, Black Dancer

Eastern Hatches

Little Red Quill, *Paraleptophlebia adoptiva:* 7–9 mm (16–20 hook); nymph, medium to dark brown; dun, reddish olive brown body, slate gray wings; spinner, dark reddish brown; 20 April–15 June; late morning to afternoon emergence, midday spinner fall; shallow gravel bottoms in slow currents; also called Slatewinged Mahogany Dun, Blue Quill, Blue Dun, Dark Blue Quill, Dark Brown Spinner, Early Blue Quill, Iron Blue Dun, May Fly Midget, Dark Dun Variant

Shadfly, *Brachycentrus spp.:* 8–12 mm (14–16 hook); nymph, dark brown case; pupa, green; adult, bright green to olive body, cream-turning-tan wing; 6–12 May; sporadic morning *(B. solomoni)* or afternoon *(B. appalachia)* emergence, evening ovipositor return; riffles w/ gravel and rubble bottoms; also called Light Shadfly *(B. appalachia)*, Dark Shadfly *(B. solomoni)*, Little Green Caddis

American March Brown, *Stenonema vicarium:* 8–12 mm (10–12 hook); nymph, brown above, light below; dun, cream and brown body, mottled olive wings; spinner, tannish to dark or olive brown body, mottled wings; 15 May–15 June, sporadic or afternoon to evening emergence, sporadic or evening spinner fall; medium to fast water over stone, gravel, or leaf-drift bottom; also called March Brown, American Brown, Gray Fox, Ginger Quill, Dark Gray Fox, Dark Cahill, Sand Drake, Great Red Spinner

Green Drake, *Ephemera guttulata:* 18–22 mm (6–12 hook); nymph, tannish gray to amber w/ olive cast; dun, creamy yellow body w/ brown marks, mottled grayish olive wings; spinner, white to light cream body w/ brown marks, mottled wings; 1–10 June, dusk to night or sporadic emergence, dusk to night spinner fall; mud banks and silt bottoms in medium to fast water; also called

Shad Fly or Shadfly, Green May, Gray Fox Variant, Large Gray Fox Variant, Shaddie, Coffin Fly or Coffinfly, Black and White Spinner, Brown and White Spinner

Eastern and Midwestern Hatches

Hendrickson, *Ephemerella subvaria:* 9–12 mm (12–14 hook); nymph, dark brown; dun, brownish olive and yellow body, slate wings; spinner, reddish brown; 25 April–25 May, afternoon emergence, afternoon to evening spinner fall; swift gravelly riffles; also called Beaverkill, Bluewinged Hendrickson, Borcher's, Red Quill, Lady Beaverkill, Brown Hen Spinner

Sulphur, *Ephemerella dorothea:* 6–9 mm (16–18 hook); nymph, freckled olive or yellowish brown; dun, yellow or yellowish orange body w/ light yellowish gray wings; spinner, yellowish brown; 20 May–5 July; afternoon to evening emergence, evening spinner fall; swift gravel runs and medium to fast riffles; also called Sulphur Dun, Sulphury Dun, Pale Evening Dun, Pale Watery Dun, Cream Variant, Small Cream Variant, Little Marryat, Brown Hen Spinner

Midwestern Hatches

Giant Michigan Mayfly, *Hexagenia limbata:* 18–33 mm (4–8 hook); nymph, amber w/ dark brown marks; dun, yellow to grayish brown body w/ purplish brown marks, olive gray wings; spinner, yellow body w/ brown marks; 25 June–20 July; emergence and spinner fall, dusk and after dark; slow, shallow streams w/ silt beds and mud banks; also called Michigan Caddis, Sandfly, Burrowing Mayfly, Fishfly, Great Olivewinged Drake, Michigan Spinner, Double Hen-wing Spinner, Extended-body Impala-wing Fly

Rocky Mountain Hatches

Brown Drake, *Ephemera simulans:* 10–14 mm (10–12 hook); nymph, amber to pale dirt gray w/ brown markings; dun, grayish yellow body w/ brown markings, gray wings w/ brown markings; spinner, body brown above, yellow below, brownish black markings on wings; 22 May–20 June; medium to fast streams w/ mixed sand and gravel; also called Chocolate Dun, March Brown.

Grasshoppers, Families Acrididae and Tettigoniidae: Various sizes, shapes, colors; not really a hatch, but present in streamside or emergent vegetation in all warm months; popular grasshopper-imitating flies include Humpies, Goofus Bugs, Crazy Goof, Letort Hopper, Deer Hoppers, Elk-hair Hoppers, Joe's Hopper, Meadow Grasshopper, Yellowbodied Grayback

Western (Rocky Mountain to West Coast) Hatches

Salmon Fly, *Pteronarcys californica:* 38–44 mm (4–10 hook); nymph, dark slate brown; adult, ribbed brown and orange body, pale gray veined wings; 1 May–30 July; late morning emergence, especially in 55–58°F water, afternoon and evening spinner fall; boulders w/ detritus; also called Giant Stonefly, Bird's Stonefly Nymph, Western Salmonfly, Lumbering Salmonfly.

Pale Morning Duns, *Ephemerella spp.,* esp. *E. infrequens, E. inermis, E. lacustris:* 5–7 mm (16–22 hook); nymph, medium to dark brown or olive brown (sometimes w/ lighter marks); dun, creamish to bright yellow body w/ olive cast, light gray wings (sometimes w/ yellowish tinges on leading edges); spinner, creamish tan to yellowish brown or olive; early June into August; slow to fast currents w/ gravel bottoms, quiet runs, still waters; also called Beaverkill, Pale Morning Spinner, Olive Quill, Rusty Spinner *(E. infrequens),* Pale Morning Olive *(E. inermis)*

Bluewinged Olives, *Baetis spp. & Pseudocloeon spp.:* 4–10 mm (14–24 hook); nymph, olive brown to blackish brown; dun, gray to olive or olive brown body, light to medium gray or reddish brown wings; spinner, varied, from light through rusty olive brown to dark brown (sometimes w/ creamish bands); hatches occur across the season, but especially June and July; sporadic emergence, but generally evening or overcast days, evening spinner falls; slow to fast currents w/ shallow gravel runs, submerged vegetation; also called Blue Dun, Light Blue Dun, Little Blue Dun, Rusty Spinner; Light Rusty Spinner, Little Iron Blue Quill, Dark Rusty Spinner *(B. tricaudatus),* Tiny Bluewinged Olive *(P. anoka, P. edmundsi);* Minute Graywinged Olive *(P. anoka);* Dark Bluewinged Olive, Dark Graywinged Olive, Minute Bluewinged Olive *(B. flavistriga);* Little Bluewinged Rusty Dun, Little Slatewinged Brown Quill *(B. brunneicolor);* Little Graywinged Brown Quill *(B. intercalaris);* Little Medium Olive Dun *(B. pygmaeus);* Little Slatewinged Olive Quill *(B. propinquis);* Dark Brown Dun, Dark

Brown Spinner *(B. hageni);* Minute Graywinged Watery *(P. fu-tile);* Pale Graywinged Olive *(B. adonis);* Pale Olive Dun *(B. bi-caudatus)*

Western Green Drake, *Drunella grandis:* 14–16 mm (8–12 hook); nymph, dark to blackish brown; dun, medium olive green body w/ lighter ribs or dark brown rings, dark slate gray wings; spinner, dark olive green to brown body w/ pale margins; 15 June–15 July; late morning to midday emergence, spinner fall at night; slow to medium currents with rocky or gravel runs; also called Green Drake, Great Leadwinged Olive Drake, Dark Morning Olive, Olive Spinner, Great Red Spinner, Prickleback (nymph)

TROLLING

Trolling is perhaps the most effective of all forms of angling. It is also one of the most boring. But it allows you to cover a lot of water and structure. And if you are using a flasher, chart recorder, temperature probe, pH meter, or some other electronic device to locate fish, at least trolling allows you to fish while you are underway. For some fish—pelagic gamefish, for example—trolling is about the only practical method of angling.

TROLLING PATTERNS

Trolling with one or two rods is easy. But when you get up to four or six lines out, you must use some sort of trolling pattern. (Here I am referring to the pattern of lines behind the boat, not the navigational trolling pattern. On this latter subject, there are almost as many theories as trollers. A thing worth keeping in mind: On a turn, the lures on the inside of the turn will run slower and the ones on the outside, faster. This enables you to vary a lure's speed without changing the boat's throttle setting. It also causes the slowed-down lures to run deeper if they are sinking lures and shallower if they are floaters. So, most trolling maneuvers are based on curves or zigzags, not straight lines.)

Standard trolling patterns have evolved over the years, and they are diagrammed below. The exact shape of the pattern isn't important, but the principles upon which all the patterns are based are important to know.

Varying line lengths accomplishes two things: (1) It puts lures varying distances behind the boat and in relation to the prop wash and hull wake; fish react to these things differently. (2) Lines that are staggered are less likely to become tangled in the turns. Notice that, in all patterns, the center line is the longest or shortest. That is important to keep lines from tangling. And, if you are fishing at different depths, the center line should also be the deepest one.

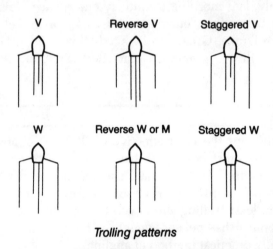

Trolling patterns

If you mix types of lines in a trolling pattern—monofilament, braided, leadcore, wire—you are looking for trouble. Each of these types of lines has a different density and water resistance, and therefore behaves differently, especially in the turns. If you must mix lines, try to keep the most dissimilar types far apart.

TROLLING SPEEDS

Trolling speed can be important because of variations in the mobility of fish. Some are swift and restless, others are slow and lethargic. And it makes a difference what kinds of prey the target species are used to feeding on. Most of the time, your trolling speed will be approximating a fish's cruising speed or the speed of the prey it is likely looking for. Sometimes, though, it is necessary to troll faster than that to get a fish's attention, to trigger its competitive instincts, to make it think it has stumbled upon a school of baitfish in alarmed flight.

Many anglers have discovered that it may be most efficient trolling at the high end of the preferred speed range for a species, and perhaps even somewhat faster than that, until fish are located. Then trolling speeds can usually be slowed, once the fish have been located and are starting to feed.

Some fishing boats are equipped with speedometers or trolling-speed indicators, but most anglers use RPM settings when discussing trolling speeds. Because such numbers are meaningless when applied to other boats, it is necessary to discuss trolling speeds in knots or miles per hour. Unfortunately, saltwater trollers tend to use knots, while inland freshwater fishermen prefer to talk in statute miles per hour. And there are other differences between them as well.

What a freshwater angler might consider a fairly fast trolling speed, a bluewater big-game fisherman would consider downright slow. Terminology varies from place to place, but we might hazard this little trolling-speed lexicon:

Speed Description	Freshwater	Saltwater
Slow (low speed)	0–2 mph	0–4 knots
Moderate (medium speed)	2–3	4–8
Fast (high speed)	3+	10+
Very Fast (ultra high speed)	5–6	12–22

Ultra-high-speed saltwater trolling is also known as passage trolling. It is, in effect, incidental trolling while making passage from one point to another or from port to fishing ground.

You won't have trouble finding experts who will dispute the exact numbers assigned above, but they will probably be in the ballpark. Frank Johnson, whose MoldCraft lures rival Sevenstrand's for preeminence in the bluewater fleets, points out that the nature of the bait affects a troller's perception of the speed. He suggests the following criteria:

Bait	Slow	Medium	Fast	Ultra High Speed
Live Bait	0–4 kt	n.a.	n.a.	n.a.
Dead Bait	2–6	4–8 kt	8–12 kt	n.a.
Artificial Lure	4–6	6–10	8–12	12–22 kt

How a bait is rigged (whether for swimming or skipping), and the performance characteristics of a lure also affect the optimum speed.

The Luhr Jensen catalog offers some advice on trolling speeds that points up how the specific nature of a lure affects the appropriate speed. These are the speeds recommended in the catalog for five different Luhr Jensen salmon lures:

J-Plug	1.9–2.1 knots
Northport Nailer Spoon	1.8–1.9
Andy Reeker Spoon	1.6–1.7
Flutter Spoon	1.5–1.6
Herring Dodger	1.3–1.4 kt for lake trout; to 1.6 kt for salmon

I doubt the company really expects its customers to be all that precise as to trolling speeds, but lists the numbers to show how each lure's optimum speed varies from the others'.

Most freshwater fish are trolled at slow to medium speeds, one to two miles per hour. Pike, salmon, trout, and striped bass can be trolled a bit faster than that (two to three mph), and brown trout and muskies are virtual speed demons (up to six mph for muskies). Among saltwater species, the range of preferred trolling speeds is much greater. Frank Johnson says that recent experience suggests that eight knots is the magic number. "If you aren't sure what fish are around, or what they are feeding on," he says, "try trolling at eight to ten knots."

The following recommended trolling speeds were compiled from information and advice gathered from numerous sources.

RECOMMENDED TROLLING SPEEDS FOR VARIOUS SALTWATER SPORT SPECIES

Saltwater Sportfish	Knots
Billfish	
Black Marlin	0–6, bait; 5–12, lures
Blue Marlin	4–6, bait; 5–10, lures
Striped Marlin	3–5, bait; 5–10, lures
White Marlin	3–5, bait; 4–8, lures
Sailfish	0–6
Spearfish	0–6
Swordfish	0–4
Drums	
Black Drum	2–3
Red Drum	2–3
White Seabass	0–3

Saltwater Sportfish	Knots
Spotted Seatrout	0–3
Weakfish	0–3
Jacks	
Amberjacks	0–6
California Yellowtail	8–12
Rainbow Runner	2–4
Mackerel	
Atlantic	4–12
King	2–6
Spanish	4–12
Wahoo	5–12
Salmon and Trout	
Chinook	0–3
Chum	0–3
Coho	0–3
Pink	0–3
Sockeye	0–3
Steelhead	0–3
Sharks	
Hammerheads	0–5
Mako	3–7
Porbeagle	0–5
Thresher	0–5
White	0–3
Tunas	
Albacore	5–12
Bigeye	5–12
Blackfin	5–12
Bluefin	3–10
Bonitos	6–12
Kawakawa	5–12
Little Tunny	5–12
Skipjack	5–12
Yellowfin	5–12
Other Saltwater Sportfish	
Barracudas	4–8
Bluefish	3–7+
Cobia	0–4
Dolphin	5–15
Groupers	0–3
Pollock	0–3
Snook	0–3
Striped Bass	0–6
Tarpon	0–4

NAVIGATION BY DEAD RECKONING

Unless you have a Loran C or know how to use a sextant, you are probably a seat-of-the-pants navigator. So long as you stay within sight of shore, have good, up-to-date charts and maps, and fish in waters that have easily identified landmarks along the shoreline, plain map-reading is probably good enough. But if you venture even a little way offshore, or the weather socks in, or the shoreline is mostly unbroken forest, or your charts are last season's—in other words, much of the time—you had better learn the rudiments of dead-reckoning navigation.

Dead reckoning, or DR, is a method of calculating a boat's position on a chart from its last accurately determined position, taking into account the courses steered, the time spent underway, and speeds through the water. The DR track is only theoretical: the path the boat would follow through the water if there were no wind, waves, current or steering error.

Even though DR's accuracy leaves something to be desired, it is *the* basic method of navigation from which all good sailors make corrections and adjustments from other sources of information (map-reading, Loran, radar, sextant, radio, and the like). Even if your boat is loaded with electronics, it's better than merely a good idea to maintain DR tracks on your charts. For one thing, it's faster than trying to keep up with changing Loran readouts; for another, it may be your only salvation in case something goes wrong with your electronic gear.

For dead reckoning to work, it is necessary that it be begun from a *known* position. In other words, start your first DR plot of the day when you leave the dock in the morning. If you start from a guesstimated position, your dead-reckoning position later in the day won't be worth a whole heck of a lot.

During the course of navigating around your fishable waters, make periodic corrections (if possible) in your estimated positions from other sources, including triangulated line-of-sight fixes on things like navigation buoys, lighthouses, and daymarks, obvious landmarks.

The Three Basic Principles of Dead Reckoning

1. A DR track is *always* begun from a known position.
2. Only true courses are steered. (Do not try to correct for wind, waves, or current.)

3. Speed through the water is used for determining distance traveled. (If you have one of those gadgets that measures air speed, *don't* use it for DR.)

The Basic Dead Reckoning Formula   **D = S × T/60**

In this formula,

D = Distance in miles (statute miles, if speed is measured or estimated in miles per hour)

S = Speed in miles per hour or knots (depending upon whether you want your distances plotted in statute or nautical miles)

T = Time in minutes

In other words, the formula can be expressed as Distance equals Speed multiplied by Time, divided by 60.

The mathematical corollaries—

$$S = 60 × D/T \text{ and } T = 60 × D/S$$

may be useful at various times, especially the former.

Sighting the landmarks   Plotting the lines of sight

—Your position is in the middle of this triangle.

Plotting position by line-of-sight and triangulation

CALCULATING BOAT SPEED FROM THROTTLE SETTINGS

On a clear day when winds and waves are low, currents are nil, and you are boating against a well-known shoreline, you can use the dead-reckoning formula to calculate your speed through the water according to various throttle settings.

Running at a constant throttle setting (and speed) parallel to the shoreline, time how long it takes to run from a point abreast of one known landmark to a point abreast of a second known landmark. If you know the precise distance between them, fine; otherwise, calculate it from your navigation chart or map. Then, use the formula

$$S = 60 \times D/T$$

to calculate your actual speed through the water, and record the answer. Repeat the same thing for various other throttle settings.

If you have a gauge that measures actual engine speed, record your calculated boat speeds as direct functions of engine speed in RPMs. This is the most accurate way to calculate speed through the water. However, if your throttle has detentes (fixed positions) or visual markings, record those settings, and you will be accurate enough. If your throttle doesn't have any sort of setting indicators, use a paint brush, waterproof marker, or file to make some.

Once you have calculated your speed-to-throttle-setting equivalencies, print them neatly on a small card and have it laminated or otherwise waterproofed. And keep it handy for easy reference while navigating by dead reckoning.

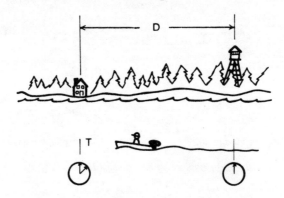

Using dead reckoning to calculate boat speed

TACKLE

ROD SENSITIVITY

Rod sensitivity is a much misunderstood subject. Mention the term, and most anglers assume you are talking about ability to feel soft strikes or nibbles through the rod. Yes, increased sensitivity does increase one's ability to perceive tiny pressures on the other end of the line. But the chief thing is, increased rod sensitivity improves casting.

If material is more sensitive for the same strength, it can be made finer. And the finer and lighter the rod, the less effort it takes to get the same results. Expend the same effort as before, and you will cast farther. Why? Partly because the more sensitive, finer material offers less wind resistance and you either get more tip speed for the same effort or the same tip speed for less effort.

Another benefit from increased sensitivity: You can fish lighter lines, and therefore cast lighter lures. The rule of thumb is, the faster the tip action, the lighter the line. Remember when you used to see a lot of UFT, ultra-fast-taper, rods in catalogs? That was before boron, before graphite, before improved fiberglass, so-called S-glass. To get that fast tip speed, without scaling down the whole rod, the butt section was made beefy (for fighting fish) and then the rod tapered down very fast to a fine tip (for casting). The result was a multipurpose rod that worked very well in the hands of a highly skilled angler.

But, for really good casting performance, you want a rod with parabolic action. A rod with a stout butt and an ultra-fast-taper tip does not flex parabolically. In the past, though, there wasn't any other alternative to casting light weights on a rod that had lots of backbone.

Today, you get better rods with better performance by substituting stronger, lighter, more sensitive materials. How much more sensitive are today's rod materials? According to Jerry Gomber, who was then product manager for Shimano American Corporation, the rod materials rank this way on a sensitivity scale of 1 to 10, assuming a uniformly high quality and optimum percentage of fibers:

Greenheart Wood	1
Split Bamboo	3
Fiberglass	3
S-Glass	5–6
Graphite	8–9
Boron	10

Before you try to make too much out of those numbers, know that, as engineers actually measure sensitivity, S-glass is 10 to 15 times more sensitive than regular fiberglass, graphite is 8 to 10 times more sensitive than S-glass (120 times more sensitive than ordinary fiberglass), and boron is 15 times more sensitive than graphite.

Sensitivity is the speed with which a vibration travels through a given material. Its frequency and amplitude are both taken into account in the measurement, from their input at the rod tip to their output at the butt. Some materials—particularly the porous ones, like wood—have an inherent tendency to dampen vibrations as they travel through the material. Others—like boron, with its long, solid tungsten filaments—transmit vibrations without much dampening of either amplitude or frequency.

Increased sensitivity is achieved at some cost in strength or durability, however. As many a rueful angler knows, boron and graphite are more brittle than fiberglass. In contemporary advertising parlance, they are less "forgiving." Consequently, many rod designers believe that composite rods are the wave of the future. By blending materials, most of the increased sensitivity of one material can be achieved without sacrificing much of the other material's durability.

BUILDING SPINNING RODS FROM FLY-ROD BLANKS

If you want to build a steelhead "noodle" rod, or just a long, supple ultralight to medium-action spinning rod, you might want to consider using a fly-rod blank. However, since fly rods are rated by line weight, rather than by lure weight or action, you might have trouble selecting the right blank. Knowing that fly lines are sized according to their weight in grains (see page 79), and that there are 437.5 grains to the ounce, it is possible to estimate a fly rod's lure-casting capability:

Fly Line Rating	Casting Weight
1	⅛ oz
2	3/16
3	⅕–¼
4	¼
5	5/16–⅓
6	⅜
7	⅖–7/16
8	½
9	9/16
10	⅝–⅔
11	¾
12	⅞

SETTING REEL DRAGS

Drag settings are very important in fishing unless you go after bluegills with bluefin-tuna tackle. When a fish has to strip line off a reel against the drag's resistance, it takes some of the fight out of him. Good fish-fighting techniques and intelligent drag settings are what enable skillful anglers to whip huge fish on light tackle.

How tight should a drag be set? The answer depends upon a lot of things—the size and fighting abilities of the fish, the weight of the tackle, the presence or absence of aquatic hazards such as submerged brush or weedbeds, and the ability and preference of the angler.

It is better to set the drag too light rather than too heavy, for several reasons: Knots, even good knots properly tied, weaken a line to some degree. Most reel drags don't start smoothly; instead, they allow too much tension to build up before working. The flexure of the rod adds to the effective resistance you can offer a fighting fish. And as the line strips off the reel and the diameter of the spooled line decreases, the actual stress on the line increases. So, if you have your reel drag set too close to the line's breaking point, a sudden rush, a bad move with the rod, or a long run can suddenly cause the knotted line to part.

As a rule, drags should be set at ¼ to ½ *the breaking strength* of the line, with ⅓ strain being a happy medium. In other words, if you are bass-fishing with balanced tackle and 15-pound-test line, your drag ought to be set at about 5 pounds, 4 to 8 pounds being the safe extremes.

Experienced anglers develop a "feel" for their tackle, and can set drags just by pulling the line with one hand and thumbing the drag wheels with the other. Truly expert anglers tend to use a spring scale as outlined below. They know that "feel" can be misleading, especially when switching from one outfit to another or fishing for different species under different conditions.

SETTING REEL DRAG WITH A SCALE

Tie your line directly onto the hook of a spring scale. Have a buddy hold the scale and, *with the rod tip pointing directly at the scale*, back slowly away, adjusting the reel drag so that the line will begin slipping at the desired stress. This is both easy and accurate, but it requires that you have available a spring scale and someone to read it while you back away.

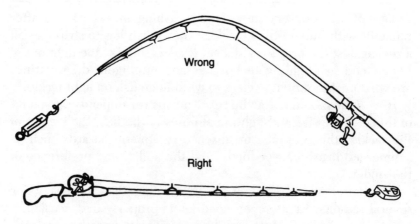

Setting reel drag with a scale

SETTING REEL DRAG WITHOUT A SCALE

If you are setting reel drags without benefit of buddy or scale, try using the system developed by the Stren people at Du Pont a few years ago. The setting won't be exact, but it will be close enough for most angling purposes:

For 6- to 10-pound-test lines: Holding the line between **thumb and little finger**, set the drag so that the reel spool barely starts rotating just before the line begins slipping between those fingers.

For 15- to 20-pound-test-lines: Use the same procedure, only this time hold the line between the **thumb and third or ring finger**.

For 25- to 45-pound-test lines: Same procedure, but use the **thumb and forefinger**.

For 50-pound-test line and above: Same procedure, using **all fingertips pressed against the palm of the hand**.

Obviously, the more strength you have in your hands, the heavier the drag setting will be, using the procedures outlined above. Once you've tried this a couple of times, you'll be able to tune your drag settings a little finer.

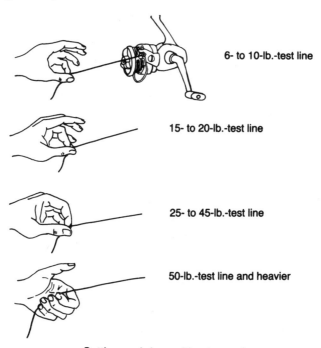

6- to 10-lb.-test line

15- to 20-lb.-test line

25- to 45-lb.-test line

50-lb.-test line and heavier

Setting reel drag without a scale

SETTING STRIKING DRAG

When trolling for saltwater game fish with lever-drag reels, it is possible to set striking as well as fighting drag. It is also highly desirable, since the initial shock of a big, powerful, speedy game fish's strike and first run can be quite extraordinary. The precise setting depends upon a lot of variable factors, such as the trolling speed of the boat, the amount of lure drag, the size of the hook, the size, speed, and striking characteristics of the most likely species. Here are the recommended ranges for each IGFA line class you are likely to use while trolling:

IGFA Class	Striking Drag
6 kg (12 lb)	1½–4 lbs
8 kg (16 lb)	2–5 lbs
10 kg (20 lb)	4–7 lbs
15 kg (30 lb)	6–9 lbs
24 kg (50 lb)	7–15 lbs
37 kg (80 lb)	15–25 lbs
60 kg (130 lb)	20–50 lbs

CALCULATING EFFECTIVELY INCREASED DRAG

When a big fish starts taking line off the reel, and you can't turn his head, what do you do? I hope you didn't say, "Tighten the drag." If you did, you are going to lose a big fish. Instead of adjusting the drag, you should use the ingenious flexure which was designed into your rod for the specific purpose of fighting a fish. And if the fish keeps taking out line, you had better consider loosening the drag. Here is why:

As line leaves a reel, the outside diameter of the line-covered spool decreases. Think of that diameter as a lever or balancing beam, you can see why it takes more effort to take out line, using a shorter lever to accomplish the same amount of work. So the drag is effectively increased, and not by just a bit.

Here is the formula:

$$X = R_1/R_2 \times D$$

X = Effective Drag (in pounds)
R_1 = Original Radius of Spool (inches)
R_2 = New Radius (inches)
D = Drag Setting (pounds)

An example: Let us say you are using a reel that, when filled with line, measured 2¼ (2.25) inches in diameter or 1⅛ (1.125) inches in radius, and you had the drag set at 3 pounds (because you are fishing 12-pound-test line). A fish takes your bait and lights out for the far horizon, taking out enough line so that the radius is now just ¾ (.75) inch. Using the above formula, X = 1.125/.75 × 3 = 4.5. In other words, your effective drag is now 4½ pounds. If it's a really tough fish and he takes the line down to a radius of just ¼ inch... forget it. You lost him because your drag exceeded your line's break load (X = 1.125/.25 × 3 = 13.5).

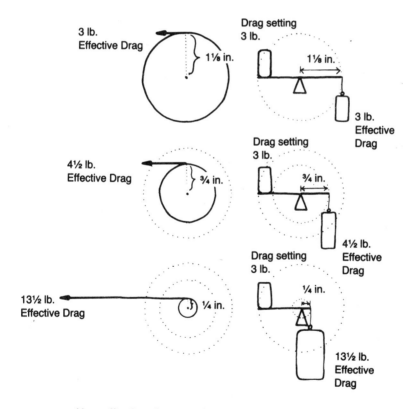

How effective diameter determines effective drag

Is it any wonder so relatively few fishermen have ever caught a fish that weighed more than their line's test strength?

REEL SPOOL CAPACITY OF LINE IN VARIOUS TEST STRENGTHS

Reel manufacturers are not very consistent when it comes to labeling the line capacities of their reels. Worse, most of them aren't even accurate. In one case, I discovered that a particular trolling reel was designed to hold 550, 600, or 800 yards of 50-pound-test line, depending upon whether I believed the manufacturer's catalog, the paperwork that came with the reel, or the label on the reel itself.

If you like to load different test strengths of line on spare spools for the same reel, you already know that some reel manufacturers are worse than others about omitting to give you much guidance in this regard. And, some of the guidance that is provided isn't worth much. For example, one manufacturer claims that one spinning reel will hold 200 yards of 4-pound-test monofilament and 500 yards of 2-pound-test, while another reel in the catalog will hold 210 yards of 4-pound-test line, but only 230 yards of 2-pound-test. Do they really expect us to believe that changing lines in one case will result in a 150 percent increase in capacity, while the other one will give us only 9.5 percent more line capacity? This is a particularly blatant case of mislabeling, but this sort of sloppiness is not uncommon.

A word in defense of the manufacturers, though. As you will see elsewhere in this book, not all lines of the same labeled test strength are actually of the same diameter. And the tension used in loading the reel will also greatly affect capacity.

Trying to make your own calculations is not easy. The precise geometry of the reel spool makes a big difference in line capacity. (Does the spool in cross section look like an **H** or a pair of **U**'s or **V**'s?) And I haven't found anyone yet who can figure out the mathematics to calculate line capacity. Or how to measure the spool geometry accurately.

If you have a line metering device, a bunch of spare spools, and a lot of time to kill, you can accurately measure the line capacities of your particular reels. If, however, you don't happen to have all three of these, the best you can do is make an intelligent guess. And you have to start somewhere. Starting with the line-capacity figures supplied by the manufacturers in their catalogs and on their reels, I averaged the increases and decreases in spool capacity when switching lines. Then I rounded off the averages to produce the chart that follows.

To use the chart, find the applicable pair of test strengths in the lefthand column. One figure represents the known capacity of your reel in a given line strength; the other figure represents your test strength of the line you want to load. Because of some rather significant differences in spool geometry between the various types of reels, I have computed capacity differences for spincast, spinning, baitcasting, and trolling reels. The listed figures are percentage changes in line capacity. If you are increasing line strength from the known capacity of the lighter line, use the negative figure. If you are calculating the capacity of the lighter line, use the positive figure. Remember, these are only approximations.

ESTIMATING LINE CAPACITY OF VARIOUS LINES AND TYPES OF REELS

Lines lb-lb	Spincast mono + %/ − %	Spinning mono + %/ − %	Casting mono + %/ − %	Jig/Troll mono + %/ − %	Trolling braid + %/ − %
2–4	—	+75/ − 33	—	—	—
4–6	+40/ − 30	+40/ − 30	+33/ − 25	—	—
6–8	+33/ − 25	+40/ − 25	+40/ − 33	—	—
8–10	+25/ − 20	+33/ − 25	+40/ − 30	—	—
8–12	+50/ − 33	+50/ − 33	+75/ − 40	—	—
10–12	+20/ − 15	+25/ − 20	+25/ − 20	—	—
10–15	+40/ − 30	+50/ − 33	+40/ − 30	—	—
12–15	+25/ − 20	+25/ − 20	+25/ − 20	+25/ − 20	—
12–17	+40/ − 30	+50/ − 33	+50/ − 33	—	—
12–20	+67/ − 40	+75/ − 40	+75/ − 40	+40/ − 30	—
15–17	+12/ − 10	+25/ − 20	+33/ − 25	—	—
15–20	+33/ − 25	+40/ − 30	+40/ − 30	+33/ − 25	—
17–20	+25/ − 20	+20/ − 15	—	+33/ − 25	—
20–25	+40/ − 30	+25/ − 20	+25/ − 20	+25/ − 20	—
20–30	—	+50/ − 33	—	+50/ − 30	+33/ − 25
25–30	—	+20/ − 15	—	+20/ − 15	—
30–40	—	+40/ − 25	—	+33/ − 25	—
30–50	—	—	—	+70/ − 40	+70/ − 40
40–50	—	—	—	+30/ − 20	—
50–60	—	—	—	+25/ − 20	—
50–80	—	—	—	+67/ − 40	+50/ − 33
80–130	—	—	—	+50/ − 33	+40/ − 25
Lines	Spincast	Spinning	Casting	Jig/Troll	Trolling

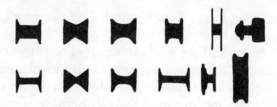

Spool geometry

A MATHEMATICAL METHOD OF ESTIMATING
LINE CAPACITY

Given its margin of error, the above chart works fine if I have anticipated the line switch you want to make. But what if you want to switch from, say, 30 pounds to 12 pounds? An unlikely transition, I admit, but you might do that if you decided to go after a 12-pound (6-kg) world record and wanted to have plenty of line capacity to whip a really brawny fish. There is a formula that was used by Harlan Major in his pioneering 1939 book, *Salt Water Fishing Tackle*.

$$C = WC/LT$$

C = Capacity of reel in desired line test
WC = Working Capacity (known capacity × known test strength)
LT = Line Test of the line you want to use

Continuing with our example above: Let us say you want to use that 12-pound-test line on a reel that is known to hold 450 yards of 30-pound-test line. So, we multiply 450 times 30 (13,500) and divide by 12 to get a new capacity of 1,125 yards of 12-pound-test line, plenty of line for battling that record fish. But wait! If you are going after a world record, it had better be a 6-kg *class* line. Our formula works with any units, so long as they are consistent. This time we call our 30-pound line a 15-kg line, so the formula is 450 × 15 / 6 and we get 1,125 yards. Plus or minus maybe 10 to 15 percent, of course.

SPOOL CAPACITY:
MONOFILAMENT VS. BRAIDED DACRON

Because of differences in stretch and compressibility between the two lines, identical reels loaded to capacity with nylon monofilament and braided hollow-core Dacron line won't have *exactly* the same amount of line on them. The differences between the two types of lines probably aren't so significant as the differences between brands or between the amounts of tension applied by two different anglers when loading the reels, but it may be interesting to note that the difference reverses itself in the heavy-weight tests. This is because the greater compressibility of the braided linen becomes relatively more important in heavier lines and on reels of such large capacity.

Line	Capacity Difference
20 lb	+5% monofilament
30 lb	+7.5% monofilament
50 lb	+7.5% monofilament
80 lb	+3% braided Dacron
130 lb	+5% braided Dacron

Note that, while most braided Dacron lines are essentially alike in terms of compressibility and "effective diameter," there are differences among braided lines. Solid-core braids are not as compressible, so a reel will probably always hold more monofilament. Cortland's braided Micron line is finer than Dacron, so a reel's capacity will be increased. And old-fashioned braided nylon squidding line is bulkier than either Micron or Dacron, but not so bulky as solid-core braids.

LINE AND BACKING CAPACITY OF FLY REELS

Unfortunately, I cannot find any mathematical method of estimating the backing capacity of fly reels, when you switch line weight or tapers. There is only one way to do it, and it requires that you have an empty spare spool available for the reel:

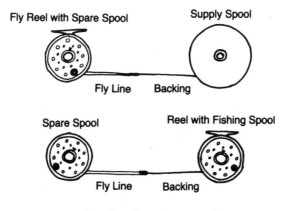

Loading fly reel to capacity

Put the fly line on first, then put the backing on top of it. (Don't fill it to full capacity under living-room conditions; under actual fishing conditions you will find your fly line going on the reel much looser and more unevenly.) Then remove the reverse-loaded spool, and put an empty spool on the reel. Now, wind the backing and fly line onto the second spool in proper order (backing first, line next).

When you see capacity figures listed for fly reels, keep these principles in mind. Lines of different tapers affect the reel's capacity. In descending order of capacity (the first line listed will accommodate the least capacity), the lines rank as follows:

1. Level
2. Double Taper
3. Weight-Forward
4. Saltwater Taper/Bass-Bug Taper
5. Shooting Taper

Shooting tapers are not complete fly lines, hence the extra capacity. They are, in effect, only the front end of a saltwater-taper fly line, behind which a monofilament or braided shooting line is attached.

Remember, too, that the strength and type of backing also affects capacity. The finest (that is, the thinnest) backing material is Cortland's braided Micron. Next comes braided Dacron, then braided nylon squidding line, and monofilament.

LINES AND LEADERS

Perhaps because there are no moving parts, lines and leaders don't get the attention they deserve from fishermen. You don't have to oil or dissemble them. They don't make noises to warn you when something is wrong. And most of the time they work just fine. But lines and leaders are more important than rods and reels in most types of angling.

Of all the things that *could* be quantified about fishing lines and leaders, figures aren't readily available for some and for others the available figures don't always make practical angling sense. The physical properties of lines and leaders easiest to quantify in terms that are immediately useful to fishermen are diameters and break-

TYPICAL TEST-STRENGTHS (LBS) OF VARIOUS TYPES OF FISHING LINES AND LEADER MATERIALS COMPARED BY DIAMETER

Diam.	Nylon	Wire Leaders		Solid Wire Trolling Lines			1x3/1x7 Stranded	Diam.
(in.)	Mono	St St	Piano	St St	Monel	Copper	St St	(mm)
0.004	1	—	—	—	—	—	—	0.10
.005	2	—	—	—	—	—	—	.13
.006	2	—	—	—	—	—	—	.15
.007	4	—	—	—	—	—	—	.18
.008	4	—	—	—	—	—	8	.20
.009	6	—	—	—	—	—	—	.23
.010	8	—	—	—	—	—	12	.25
.011	8–10	27	28	—	—	—	18	.28
.012	10	32	34	—	—	—	20–25	.31
.013	12	38	39	—	10	—	—	.33
.014	12–14	44–54	46	—	—	—	—	.36
.015	14–17	—	—	—	—	—	30–40	.38
.016	15–20	58–61	60	20	—	—	—	.41
.017	17–20	—	—	—	—	—	—	.43
.018	20–25	69–72	76	25	20	—	45–60	.46
.020	25	86–88	90–93	30	25	—	—	.51
.021	25–30	—	—	—	—	—	60	.53
.022	30–33	95–108	114	35	30	—	—	.56
.023	30–40	—	—	40	—	—	—	.58
.024	40	119–124	136	50	35	—	90–100	.61
.025	45	—	—	—	40	18–20	—	.64
.026	50	135–140	156–159	—	—	—	—	.66
.027	—	—	—	—	—	—	135	.69
.028	—	—	184	60	50	—	—	.71
.029	55	174–184	198	60–65	—	25	—	.74
.030	50–60	—	212	—	60	—	140	.76
.031	50–60	195	226	—	—	—	—	.79
.032	66	—	240	75	60	28–30	—	.81
.033	—	213–218	250–256	85	—	30	170	.84
.034	66–77	—	282	—	—	—	—	.86
.035	77–80	225–258	288	—	75	—	—	.89
.036	—	—	—	100	—	37–40	175	.91
.037	—	250–267	322	—	—	—	—	.94
.038	88	—	—	—	—	—	—	.97
.039	—	—	—	—	—	—	200–250	.99
.040	—	—	—	—	100	—	—	1.02
.041	90	280–330	—	—	—	—	—	1.04
.043	100	300–360	—	—	—	—	—	1.09
.045	110	315–397	—	—	—	—	—	1.14
.047	120	—	—	—	—	—	—	1.19
.048	130	—	—	—	—	—	—	1.22

NOTE: Coated wire and 49-strand aircraft cable are handled in "Brand Differences in Cable Lines and Leaders," on page 74 below.

ing strengths. Diameter and breaking strength are measurable, comparable, and important.

Diameter affects a line's visibility and sink rate, the ease with which and how far it can be cast, how much sinker weight will be required to hold bottom or a given trolling depth, how much line you can put on a reel, even how well a knot will hold.

Breaking strength (or break load) affects your choice of rod, how much drag you set on the reel, and how much muscle you can put into the fight.

MONOFILAMENT FISHING LINE

Probably because so few line manufacturers list line diameters on their spool labels, most anglers buy monofilament line according to test strengths. (Fly-fishermen buying monofilament leader and tippet material are an exception to this rule.) Yet few fishermen actually know how strong their lines are; they read what the labels say. And manufacturers do not think alike when it comes to sticking test-strength labels on their fishing lines.

Before trying to draw too many conclusions from the raw numbers listed below, better consider these points:

Minute differences in diameter may or may not make an actual fishing difference. If reel capacity is a problem, or you want to hold bottom in a current with the lightest possible sinker, then an otherwise unimportant difference may help you select the proper line.

Most monofilament lines are rated by pound test, more or less a guarantee that they will not break when stressed up to the listed test strength. Most will not break until considerably overstressed, a safety factor to accommodate the average angler's poor knots.

All figures—diameters and breaking strengths—were supplied by the manufacturers. Except where noted, average actual breaking strengths listed are based on tests of dry monofilament line.

DIAMETER AND BREAKING STRENGTH OF SELECTED PREMIUM MONOFILAMENT LINES

DIAMETER IN INCHES/AVERAGE ACTUAL BREAK LOAD IN POUNDS

Lbs. Test	Ande (Pink)	Garcia*	Maxima*	Sigma	Stren*	Trilene XL	Trilene XT
2	.006	.005	.005	.005	.005	.005	.007
	2.9	2.2	x.x	2.4	2.5	3.3	5.5
4	.008	.008	.007	.007	.007	.007	.008
	8.6	4.2	x.x	4.9	4.9	5.5	7.2
6	.010	.009	.009	.009	.009	.008	.010
	10.9	6.2	x.x	7.2	7.1	7.5	10.2
8	.011	.011	.010	.011	.010	.010	.012
	10.1	8.2	x.x	9.8	9.4	10.7	15.3
10	.012	.013	.012	.013	.012	.012	.013
	12.9	10.2	x.x	11.5	11.9	13.3	18.8
12	.014	.014	.013	.013	.013	.013	.014
	15.2	12.2	x.x	14.3	14.1	16.3	21.1
14/15	.016	.015	.015	.015	.014	.013	.015
	19.6	14.2	x.x	19.4	16.5	18.4	23.7
17	NA	.016	NA	.017	.016	.015	.017
	NA	17.2	NA	20.3	20.2	22.2	29.7
20	.018	.018	.017	.018	.018	.016	.019
	24.4	20.2	xx.x	24.1	24.1	26.0	35.5
25	.020	.020	.020	.021	.020	.018	.021
	30.2	25.2	xx.x	29.3	29.3	32.9	43.3
30	.022	.022	.022	.023	.026	.020	.022
	35.6	30.2	xx.x	35.6	35.3	37.6	46.8
50	.028	.028	.028	.030	.029	.027	.027
	50.2	50.2	xx.x	66.0	59.7	62.6	62.6
80	.035	.036	.035	.039	.039	.035	.035
	88.4	80.2	xx.x	94.0	97.0	99.3	99.3
130	.051	NA	.051	.051	NA	NA	.048
	130.1	NA	xxx.x	150.0	NA	NA	170.7

*Notes:

A **Garcia** spokesman says that both Gladiator and Royal Bonnyl II are identical in diameter and breaking strength, differing only in hardness and limpness. Abu-Garcia supplied manufacturing standards, rather than actual breaking strengths. **Maxima** was unable to furnish actual breaking strengths. **Stren** is not tested wet or dry, but "conditioned": exposed to optimum laboratory conditions (temperature 72°F, relative humidity 50 percent) until the line reaches equilibrium with the laboratory atmosphere.

HOW WATER AFFECTS MONOFILAMENT LINE

Before we begin, a few definitions:

Modulus: Short for **Modulus of Elasticity**, also known as modulus of flexure or beam stiffness. A measure of a line's relative limpness or stiffness, it is the amount of force required to flex a material a standard distance, measured in pounds per square inch (psi). The higher the number, the stiffer the line.

Break Load: Also known as breaking strain or break strength. (Not to be confused with test strength, which is the labeled rating and not a measured performance characteristic.) We use pounds, the rest of the world uses kilograms.

Elongation: The amount a line will stretch before it breaks, measured as a percentage of the line's length before any weight or force was applied.

Knot Strength: The break load of a *knotted* line, measured in pounds or kilograms. This is a measure of a line's ability to take knots. (Not to be confused with knot efficiency, which is a measure of a knot's tendency to weaken a line and is expressed as a percentage of the line's unknotted break load.)

Recovery: Short for **Recovery from Deformation.** Nylon has "memory," a tendency to resume its last shape, usually some sort of coil because of the way line is spooled. Recovery is a measure of a monofilament's ability to relax or "forget." (If you took a blade and slashed across a supply spool of monofilament, the line would fall to the floor in short pieces. If they landed on the floor as circles, recovery would be nil, 0 percent. If they landed as perfectly straight pieces, recovery would be complete, 100 percent.) The higher the percentage of recovery, the more manageable the line will be.

Tensile Strength: Expressed in pounds per square inch (psi), this is a measure of a material's ability to resist being torn apart under stress. (If a monofilament fishing line's cross-sectional area were 1 square inch, it would take well over 100,000 pounds or 50 tons to break it. However, a 10-pound-test line's cross-sectional area is only about 0.00011304 square inches, which is why most lines rated at 10 pounds will break at 11 to 12 pounds.)

Test Rating: Also called test strength and expressed in pounds or kilograms, this is the number that goes on the label, the manufacturer's promise to the angler that the line will not break at loads below this point. (Not to be confused with *Class Rating,* which is a promise that the line will break close to but below the IGFA class maximum allowance.)

So let's have a look at the difference water makes in monofilament fishing line:

MONOFILAMENT FISHING LINE PROPERTIES: WET VS. DRY

Property	Degree of Change	Typical 10-Pound-Test Values Dry Mono	Wet Mono
Diameter	1½ to 5%	.012 in	.01218 to .0126 in
Break Load	(18 to 22%)	12 lb	9.84 to 9.36 lb
Tensile Strength	(20 to 30%)	120,000 psi	96,000 to 84,000 psi
Elongation	40 to 55%	22%	30.8% to 34.1%
Recovery	1 to (15%)	85%	72.3% to 85.9%
Modulus	(55 to 75%)	200,000 psi	50,000 to 90,000 psi
Knot Strength			
Overhand Knot	(5 to 20%)	8 lb	6.4 to 7.6 lb
Improved Clinch	(12 to 30%)	11 lb	7.7 to 9.7 lb

NOTE: Degrees of change listed within parentheses are decreases; other changes are increases.

CLASS LINES, COMPARED

The so-called class lines, which are designed to conform to the IGFA line classes for record purposes, differ from test-strength lines in two ways. Most lines are actually a good bit stronger than their test ratings; class lines are guaranteed to break *below* the class rating. Pound tests are based on dry strength and IGFA class ratings are based on wet strength.

Let us compare two IGFA class lines—Tournament-grade Ande and Du Pont's new Stren Class—with Berkley's high-strength Trilene XT, recently relabeled as a so-called "World-Record Line." The numbers are as furnished by the manufacturers, except that in Ande's case I converted their millimeters into inches so that diameters could be better compared. Berkley and Du Pont furnished both wet and dry break loads (BL), which are interesting to compare to each other and to the IGFA maximum allowance in pounds for each class.

Berkley has relabeled Trilene XT so that each test rating is assigned to an IGFA class. This has resulted in two, and sometimes three, lines being assigned to one class. I have listed the highest-rated XT for each class in which there were choices. (I doubt that anyone wants to fish against the record book with a seriously under-strength line.) Note how close to IGFA's allowed maximums two of Berkley's wet-break-load figures are for 2-lb-test XT and 1-pound XT. For many anglers, I suspect that's too close for comfort.

CLASS LINES COMPARED BY DIAMETER AND BREAK LOAD

IGFA			Ande Tournament		Stren Class		
Class		*Max.*	*Diam*	*Dry BL*	*Diam*	*Dry BL*	*Wet BL*
Kg	*[Lb]*	*Lb*	*in*	*Lb*	*in*	*Lb*	*Lb*
1	[2]	2.20	.0049	2.0	.0058	2.6	2.0
2	[4]	4.40	.0069	4.1	.0077	4.8	4.0
4	[8]	8.81	.0098	8.3	.0111	9.4	7.8
6	[12]	13.22	.0128	13.2	.0135	15.0	12.3
8	[16]	17.63	.0148	16.4	.0153	18.6	15.5
10	[20]	22.04	.0167	21.7	.0178	24.0	19.5
15	[30]	33.06	.0207	32.0	.0218	34.7	28.0
24	[50]	52.91	.0276	52.1	NA	—	—
37	[80]	81.57	.0335	81.0	NA	—	—
60	[130]	132.27	.0472	131.8	NA	—	—

IGFA			Trilene XT			
Class		*Max.*	*Diam*	*Dry BL*	*Wet BL*	*Test*
Kg	*[Lb]*	*Lb*	*in*	*Lb*	*Lb*	*Lb*
1	[2]	2.20	.00527	2.96	2.20	1
2	[4]	4.40	.00705	5.45	4.39	2
4	[8]	8.81	.00960	10.20	8.02	6
6	[12]	13.22	.01172	15.29	11.63	8
8	[16]	17.63	.01346	18.78	14.94	10
10	[20]	22.04	.01534	23.68	18.34	14
15	[30]	33.06	.01856	35.51	28.17	20
24	[50]	52.91	.02326	51.76	42.60	40
37	[80]	81.57	.02991	76.71	60.51	60
60	[130]	132.27	.04158	126.67	100.69	80

WIRE AND WEIGHTED LINES FOR DEEP TROLLING

Wire trolling lines and wire leader materials must not be confused. Trolling wires are soft-drawn for flexibility. Stainless steel and Monel trolling wire have about the same test strength as premium monofilament of the same diameter. Wire leader material is hard-drawn. It is much stronger, stiffer, and thinner than trolling wire.

Take a quick look at the wire and lead-core trolling lines:

WIRE AND LEAD-CORE TROLLING LINES COMPARED BY STRENGTH (IN LBS.) AND DIAMETER

Diam in	Stainless Steel	Monel	Copper	Coated Lead-Core	Uncoated Lead-Core	Diam mm
0.013	—	10	—	—	—	0.33
.015	—	15	—	—	—	0.38
.016	20	20	—	—	—	0.41
.018	25	20–25	—	—	—	0.46
.020	30	25–30	—	—	—	0.51
.022	35	30–35	—	—	14	0.56
.023	40	—	—	—	—	0.58
.024	40–50	35	—	—	15	0.61
.025	40–50	40	20	—	—	0.64
.026	50	45	—	—	—	0.66
.028	60	50–60	—	—	—	0.71
.029	—	—	25	—	18	0.74
.030	65	60	—	—	18	0.76
.032	75	60–80	30	—	18–27	0.81
.034	75–85	—	—	25	27–45	0.86
.035	90	75–100	—	27	25–45	0.89
.036	100	90–100	40	30	25–45	0.91
.037	—	—	50*	30	—	0.94
.038	—	—	—	30	45	0.97
.039	—	—	—	—	60	0.99
.040	—	100	—	45	60	1.02
.041	—	—	—	45	60	1.02
.042	—	—	—	60	60	1.02
.045	—	—	—	—	60	1.14
.047	—	—	—	—	60	1.19

*NOTE: This figure is for seven-stranded copper, Weller's Coppertroll, the strongest copper trolling line that I know. All other figures in this column are for solid or single-stranded copper lines.

As you might guess from those figures in the two lead-core line columns, differences between brands can be significant.

Now look at six popular brands of lead-core lines. Four are uncoated, one (Cabela's) has a very light, lubricating finish over the braided Dacron jacket, and only Gladding's Special line comes with a bonded-plastic, fly-line-type coating.

This time, let's turn the numbers around, arranging them by test-strength rather than diameter:

COMPARING BRAND DIFFERENCES IN LEAD-CORE LINES

Test Lb	Cabela's Lead-Core	Cortland Kerplunk	Gladding		Sunset Tel-a-Depth	Weller Lead-Core	Test Lb
			Mark V	Special			
14	—	.022	—	—	—	—	14
15	—	—	—	—	.024	—	15
18	.029	.032	.030/31	.033/34	.030	.029	18
25	.032	—	.034/36	—	—	—	25
27	—	.034	—	—	.031/32	.032	27
30	—	—	—	.036/38	—	—	30
36	—	.035	—	—	.034/35	.035	36
45	.034/35	.038	.036/38	.040/42	.038	.035	45
60	—	.047	.039/41	.042/44	—	.045	60

SINK RATE OF LEAD-CORE LINES

Except for those two light-tackle lines—14-pound-test Kerplunk and Sunset's 15-pound-test Tel-a-Depth, both of which use a thinner lead core—roughly the same size lead wire is used in all lead-core lines, regardless of test strength or final diameter.

Before making any allowances for the differences in diameter noted in the preceding table, here is the way you can expect lead-core lines to stack up in terms of sink rate:

18-lb-test (fastest sinking)
14-lb
15-lb
27-lb
30-lb
36-lb
45-lb
60-lb (slowest sinking)

LEADER MATERIALS

Numerous materials have found favor among anglers in different parts of the country for different types of fishing: regular and stiff monofilament, solid and stranded wire, coated wire and cable. Each type has its place in the angler's armory, but they are not interchangeable. Besides such things as relative visibility, weight, flexibility, and manageability, some of which aren't easily quantifiable, there are the aspects of strength and diameter. These two properties of leader material are related, but they vary considerably from type to type, as can be seen below.

LEADER MATERIALS COMPARED BY STRENGTH AND DIAMETER

Diam in	Nylon Mono	Piano Wire	Solid St St	1×7 St St	Coated 1×7	7×7 Cable	Diam mm
			Typical Test Strengths (Pounds)				
0.003	1	—	—	—	—	—	0.10
.005	2	—	—	—	—	—	0.13
.008	2–6	—	—	8	—	—	0.20
.009	3–6	—	—	—	—	—	0.23
.010	4–8	—	—	12	—	—	0.25
.011	5–12	28	27	18	—	—	0.28
.012	6–12	34	32	20–27	8	—	0.30
.013	7–15	39	38	—	—	—	0.33
.014	8–15	46	44–45	—	—	—	0.36
.015	10–17	—	—	30–40	12	—	0.38
.016	12–17	60	58	—	—	—	0.41
.018	15–25	76	69–70	45–60	10–18	—	0.46
.020	20–30	90–93	86	—	27	—	0.51
.021	20–30	—	—	60	—	—	0.53
.022	20–33	114	95–105	—	—	—	0.56
.024	25–40	136	119–124	90–100	40	—	0.61
.025	25–45	—	—	—	—	60	0.64
.026	30–50	156–159	135–140	—	20–30	—	0.66
.027	30–50	—	—	135	—	—	0.69
.028	32–50	184	—	—	45	—	0.71
.029	40–55	198	174	—	—	—	0.74
.030	40–60	212	—	140	—	—	0.76

			Typical Test Strengths (Pounds)				
Diam in	Nylon Mono	Piano Wire	Solid St St	1 × 7 St St	Coated 1 × 7	7 × 7 Cable	Diam mm
.031	40–60	226	195	—	—	90	0.79
.032	40–66	240	—	—	60	—	0.81
.033	45–80	250	218	170	—	—	0.84
.034	50–85	282	—	—	60	—	0.86
.035	50–85	288	225–240	—	—	—	0.89
.036	50–85	—	—	—	—	175	0.91
.037	60–85	—	250	—	—	—	0.94
.038	60–88	—	—	200–250	80	—	0.97
.041	75–90	—	280–325	—	—	—	1.04
.043	80–100	—	300–360	—	120	—	1.09
.045	80–100	—	315–397	—	—	275	1.14
.047	90–130	—	—	—	—	—	1.19
.050	100–130	—	—	—	—	—	1.27
.052	—	—	—	—	210	275	1.32
.053	—	—	—	—	—	400	1.35
.055	120–165	—	—	—	—	—	1.40
.058	150–185	—	—	—	—	—	1.47
.063	—	—	—	—	—	400–480	1.60
.064	200	—	—	—	—	—	1.63
.068	250	—	—	—	—	—	1.73
.072	285	—	—	—	—	600	1.83
.075	—	—	—	—	250	—	1.91
.081	—	—	—	—	—	800	2.06
.084	375	—	—	—	—	—	2.13

BRAND DIFFERENCES IN CABLE LINES AND LEADERS

Let us compare the stranded-wire wares of two companies, popularly priced Berkley and top-quality Sevenstrand. Life would be simpler if we could say that one company's stranded-wire products were stronger or finer in diameter than the other's. But we can't.

Let me show you why, comparing stranded wire, nylon-coated wire, and 49-strand aircraft cable:

BERKLEY AND SEVENSTRAND CABLES, COMPARED

Diam in	Stranded Wire		Nylon-Coated		7 × 7 Cable		Diam mm
	Berkley	Sevenstr.	Berkley	Sevenstr.	Berkley	Sevenstr.	
0.008	—	8	—	—	—	—	0.20
.010	—	12	—	—	—	—	0.25
.011	—	18	—	—	—	—	0.28
.012	20	27	—	8	—	—	0.30
.015	30	40	—	12	—	—	0.38
.018	45	60	10	18	—	—	0.46
.020	—	—	—	27	—	—	0.51
.021	60	—	15	—	—	—	0.53
.024	100	90	—	40	—	—	0.61
.025	—	—	—	—	60	—	0.64
.026	—	—	20 & 30	—	—	—	0.66
.027	—	135	—	—	—	—	0.69
.028	—	—	45	—	—	—	0.71
.030	140	—	—	—	—	—	0.76
.031	—	—	—	—	90	—	0.79
.032	—	—	60	—	—	—	0.81
.034	—	—	—	60	—	—	0.86
.036	—	—	—	—	—	175	0.91
.038	—	—	80	—	135	—	0.97
.039	210	250	—	—	—	—	0.99
.042	—	—	120	—	—	—	1.07
.044	—	—	—	—	175	—	1.12
.045	—	—	—	—	—	275	1.14
.048	—	—	—	90	—	—	1.22
.052	—	—	210	—	275	—	1.32
.053	—	—	—	—	—	400	1.35
.058	—	—	—	135	—	—	1.47
.062	—	—	—	—	—	480	1.57
.063	—	—	—	—	400	—	1.60
.065	—	—	—	170	—	—	1.65
.072	—	—	—	—	600	600	1.83
.075	—	—	—	250	—	—	1.91
.081	—	—	—	—	—	800	2.06

CRIMPING SLEEVES FOR CABLE AND MONOFILAMENT

Solid or single-stranded trolling wires and wire leaders are usually fastened by means of haywire twists. But multistranded wire and cable require knotting (which is difficult), fusing with heat (in the case of nylon-coated wire), or crimping with special sleeves. Most anglers prefer to use crimp sleeves. In fact, in heavy monofilament, crimped connections are favored by some anglers over knots. A crimped connection will be sure if:

    (1)   the proper size high-quality sleeve is used,
    (2)   a good crimping tool is used,
    (3)   the crimp is made properly.

Taking them in reverse order, a proper crimp requires that the two sections of wire or monofilament remain side by side; they must not cross one another inside the sleeve. This is especially important in the case of monofilament. Several crimping tools are on the market, and a few of them are good ones, which cost upward of fifteen or twenty dollars (my favorite has always been the Sevenstrand Type C). Ordinary pliers, fishing pliers, or an electrician's crimping tool must not be used. To be really sure about sizes, you had best use the sleeves made or sold by the same company that made the wire. Unfortunately, several wire companies do not make sleeves, and of the monofilament manufacturers only Berkley makes crimping sleeves. Avoid at all costs the thin, cheap sleeves you sometimes see on the discount-store shelves.

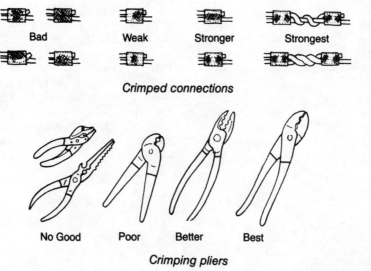

Bad   Weak   Stronger   Strongest

Crimped connections

No Good   Poor   Better   Best

Crimping pliers

CRIMPING MONOFILAMENT

I've never liked crimped connections in monofilament, because it is so easy to nick and weaken the nylon. Now, however, Sevenstrand makes excellent special monofilament leader sleeves that don't have sharp edges and that have a double hole through the middle. Because mono comes in a range of diameters for the same test strengths, it is best to use diameter rather than test strength in choosing a sleeve:

Sleeve	Mono Diam.	Test Range
AM9	.043 in	100–185 lb
AM11	.071	185–370
AM12	.085	220–440
AM14	.105	250–500

Consult the diameter/strength tables on pages 73 and 74.

Not all manufacturers of sleeves make them in the same sizes, so we had better compare some: Berkley (both copper and nickel/black), Mason Heavy Duty, and Sevenstrand.

Be sure to compare the diameters and breaking strengths of the leader materials in the table on page 73.

Because all four sleeves are sized differently, you should know these inside diameters of the Mason sleeves: size 1, .033 in; 2, .046; 3, .055; 4, .070; 6, .082; 7, .106; 8, .116; 9, .125; 10, .140; 12, .159; and 14, .203.

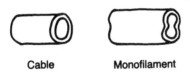

Cable   Monofilament

Crimp sleeves

A COMPARISON OF CRIMPING SLEEVES FOR WIRE & MONOFILAMENT

Sleeve Size:	1	2	3	4	5	6	7	8	9	10	11	12	14
1 × 7 Wire													
Berkley Copper	20	30	45	60–100	—	—	—	—	—	—	—	—	—
Berkley Nickel/Black	—	20–45	60–140	210	—	210	—	—	—	—	—	—	—
Mason Heavy Duty	30	45–60	90–100	125–150	—	—	210	—	—	—	—	—	—
Sevenstrand	8–27	40–60	90	135	170	250	—	—	—	—	—	—	—
Coated Wire													
Berkley Copper	—	—	10–15	20–45	—	—	—	—	—	—	—	—	—
Berkley Nickel/Black	—	10	15–45	60–80	120	210	—	—	—	—	—	—	—
Mason Heavy Duty	10	15	20–30	45–60	—	90–120	—	210	—	—	—	—	—
Sevenstrand	—	8–27	40	—	60	—	90	—	135	170	250	—	—
7 × 7 Cable													
Berkley Copper	—	—	—	—	—	—	600	—	—	—	—	—	—
Berkley Nickel/Black	—	—	60–90	135	175	275–400	—	—	—	—	—	—	—
Mason Heavy Duty	—	—	—	—	—	—	—	275	480	—	—	600	800
Sevenstrand	—	—	—	—	—	175	275	400	—	480	600	800	—
Monofilament	1	2	3	4	5	6	7	8	9	10	11	12	14
Berkley Copper	4–10	12–15	17–25	30–40	90–125	150–225	250	—	—	—	—	—	—
Berkley Nickel/Black	—	12–20	25–50	60–80	—	80	100–130	150	180	200	—	200	—
Mason Heavy Duty	10–15	20–30	30–40	50–60	—	80	100–125	150	165	185	200	220	300
Sevenstrand	—	10	15–20	30–40	50–60	—	—	—	—	—	—	—	250

FLY LINES AND LEADERS

Fly lines and leaders are different from those used in other forms of fishing, and need to be considered separately. **Fly lines**, especially, depart from the angling norm. In other forms of fishing, it is the lure, bait, sinker, or some other attached weight that pulls the line through the air on a cast. In fly-fishing, it is the weight of the line that pulls the fly or bait through the air. **Fly leaders** are made of the same monofilament (and sometimes wire) materials that are used in other types of angling, but their construction and dimensions are somewhat different.

FLY LINE DESIGNATIONS AND STANDARDS

Fly lines are not rated by strength, but by weight, taper, and function. (Most fly lines will test at 35 to 45 pounds or so, but tippets will break long before that.) **Weight** is the basic criterion, because it is the weight of the fly line that determines what sort of rod it will take to cast it well. **Taper** is the distribution of a fly line's weight, which also affects its shape in profile. **Function** is in effect a statement of the line's density, whether it is designed to float or sink.

Every fly line is assigned a designation code according to certain criteria established in 1961 by AFTMA, the American Fishing Tackle Manufacturers Association. This code replaced an earlier one based on the diameter of silk fly lines. It is a three-part code:

TAPER-WEIGHT-FUNCTION CODE

Taper		Weight	Function	
Level	L	1 through 12	F	Floating
Double Taper	DT		I	Intermediate
Weight Forward	WF		S	Sinking
Shooting Taper	ST		F/S	Floating/Sinking

FLY LINE WEIGHTS

A fly line's weight is expressed as a single number from 1 through 12, which represents the weight of the first 30 feet, exclusive of any level tip or run-in section. A line designated 6 may be referred to as a "6-weight line" or a "number 6 line." The number does not represent any units of weight, although line weights are determined by weighing the front section of line in grains (437.5 grains = 1 ounce) before a number is assigned. AFTMA sets weights, assigns numbers, and specifies acceptable manufacturing tolerances.

AFTMA FLY LINE STANDARDS

No.	Weight	Range
1	60 grains	54–66 grains
2	80	74–86
3	100	94–106
4	120	114–126
5	140	134–146
6	160	152–168
7	185	177–193
8	210	202–218
9	240	230–250
10	280	270–290
11	330	318–342
12	380	368–392

FLY LINE TAPERS

To put the casting weight where it will do the most good, fly lines are made with specific profiles. Most of them are tapered.

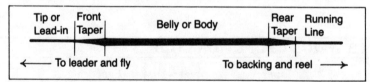

Fly-line nomenclature.

Level Line (L)

The cheapest, bulkiest, and most difficult to cast of all fly lines, the untapered level line should not be, but usually is, sold as a beginner's fly line. There is no faster way to frustrate and turn off a would-be fly-fisherman than to condemn him to fighting with a cheap rod and a level line. Level lines are available in floating and sinking versions. The level line is best suited to trolling streamer flies for landlocked salmon and lake trout, or for drifting worms or other baits downcurrent without casting.

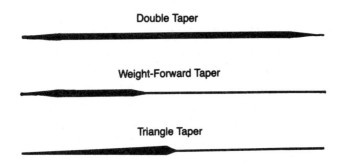

Double Taper

Weight-Forward Taper

Triangle Taper

Triangle taper compared to double-taper and weight-forward fly lines.

Double-Taper Line (DT)

The double-taper line casts well, is the easiest line to roll cast, allows for the most delicate presentations, and can be reversed when the front end begins to show signs of wear and tear. It is the all-around fly line. Available in all densities: floating, intermediate, floating/sinking, and sinking.

Weight-Forward Line (WF)

With most of its weight in the front end, the weight-forward line allows for faster and, in the hands of experts, much longer casts because the weighted front end tapers down quickly to a thinner-diameter running line. Fly presentation is not so delicate as with double-taper lines. Weight-forward lines are available in all densities. Also known as rocket or torpedo taper.

Saltwater Taper/Bass-Bug Taper (WF)

Also indentified by some manufacturers as a blunt weight-forward taper, this is a variant of the WF line, has a shorter, heavier front taper, and is used to drive bulky, air-resistant bass bugs and saltwater flies into heavy winds. Only expert casters can make delicate presentations with these tapers, but they can get off casts very quickly, with little or no false casting. Available in all densities.

Triangle Taper (TT)

This recent invention by the legendary Lee Wulff is a floating weight-forward line that features a continuous taper for the first 40 feet, then drops quickly down to a fine .032-in diameter shooting line. It doesn't load a rod as rapidly as a conventional weight-forward taper, but once the taper does clear the rod it ought to cast like a WF. The continuous taper also puts the finest part of the line nearest the fish. I haven't used this new line much, so I'll have to repeat Wulff's claims that it is "ideal for trout" because "the heavy line is constantly turning over lighter line for the most efficient use of your casting power" and that it is "the best line for roll casting or mending line." When I was fishing in Sweden recently, most of the expert fly-fishermen I met used lines of their own making or Wulff's Triangle Taper.

Shooting Taper (ST)

This 30- to 35-foot fly line is like the front end of a tapered fly line, a design that is used by experts for extremely long distance casting. Instead of using a built-in running line, it attaches to a finer, lighter monofilament or braided shooting line for a minimum of friction through the rod guides. Available in all densities except F/S. (Many fly-fishermen make their own shooting tapers by cutting fly lines down to size and whipping loops on the rear ends. You can use WF lines, but you can get two STs from one DT line.)

Fly Line Functions or Densities

Thanks to the different specific gravities of synthetic materials, fly lines can now be made in various densities, everything from high-floating lines to truly fast-sinking weighted shooting heads.

Floating (F)

Floating fly lines, which are the easiest to cast, are made with buoyant air spaces entrapped among the fibers. Some manufacturers, like Gudebrod, make their floating lines somewhat less buoyant so they will float *in* the surface film rather than on top of it. On sunny days, partly submerged lines may cast thinner shadows under water.

Intermediate (I)

Sometimes called neutral-density lines, these vary somewhat in concept, from neutrally buoyant lines to very slow sinking lines. Designed to present a fly just below the surface.

Floating/Sinking or Sink-Tip (F/S)

Most such lines are made to float except for the tip section, which is weighted to sink wet flies, streamers, and nymphs. Most F/S lines are weighted in their first 10 feet to sink at a rate of about 1½ to 2 feet per second. However, Cortland and 3M/Scientific Anglers make sink-tip lines with varying lengths of sinking tips and varying sink rates:

SINK RATES OF CORTLAND & 3M/SCIENTIFIC ANGLERS SINK-TIP LINES

Category	Tip Length	Cortland 444		3M/Scientific Anglers	
Slow	10 feet	Type #1	1.25–1.75 ips	—	—
Fast	10	—	—	Wet Tip	1.50–1.75 ips
Extra Fast	10	Type #3	3.50–4.00	Hi-D & Ultra Hi-D	2.50–4.25
Extra Fast	20	Type #3	3.50–4.00	Wet Belly	3.00–4.00
Extra Fast	30	Type #3	3.50–4.00	Wet Head	3.25–4.25
Super Fast	10	—	—	Ultra Hi-Speed Hi-D	3.75–5.25

Sinking (S)

Sinking lines are made in all sorts of densities and sink rates, which we will examine shortly.

Shooting Head (S)

Usually built around a lead core, this is in effect a weighted, ultra-fast-sinking shooting taper. In weight, they vary from about 400 to more than 800 grains. The best of them are tapered, usually with the thickest, least dense section in the butt and the finest, densest section at the tip. Some fly-fishermen make level shooting heads or shooting-head sections (located between fly line and leader butt) out of lead-core trolling line. Weighted shooting heads are very difficult and even dangerous to cast.

SINK RATES OF INTERMEDIATE AND SINKING FLY LINES

Sink rate is measured in inches per second (ips). By counting, a fisherman can have a pretty good idea how deep his fly is in slow or still water. But remember, the leader and fly are buoyant, so they will not be as deep as the fly line itself. And in flowing waters, the water resistance of the line will offset its density, so there are practical limits as to the fishing depth achievable with sinking fly lines. Here are some typical recommendations:

Intermediate	0–2 feet maximum
Slow Sinking	3–5
Fast Sinking	5–10
Extra-Fast Sinking	10–20
Super-Fast Sinking	10–30
Shooting Head	10–40

Most fly line manufacturers do not publish the sink rates of their sinking fly lines, but at least two do: Cortland and 3M/Scientific Anglers.

SINK RATES OF CORTLAND & 3M/SCIENTIFIC ANGLERS SINKING LINES

	Cortland		3M/Scientific Anglers	
Category	444	Sink Rate	Wet Cel	Sink Rate
Intermediate	Intermediate	1.15–1.50 ips	Wet Cel	1.25–1.75 ips
Slow	Type #1	1.25–1.75	Wet Cel I	1.75–2.50
Fast	Type #2	2.50–3.00	Wet Cel II	2.00–3.00
Extra Fast	Type #3	3.50–4.00	Hi-D	3.25–4.25
Super Fast	Type #4	4.25–5.00	Hi-Speed Hi-D	3.75–5.25
Shooting Head	Kerboom		Deep Water	
450 grains		7.00–8.75	Express	—
550 grains		9.50–10.25		7–8
700 grains		—		8–9
850		—		9–10

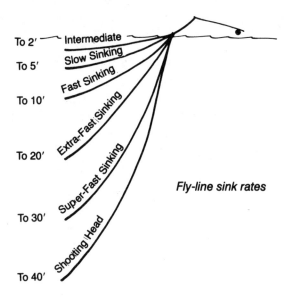

To 2' — Intermediate
To 5' — Slow Sinking
To 10' — Fast Sinking
To 20' — Extra-Fast Sinking
To 30' — Super-Fast Sinking
To 40' — Shooting Head

Fly-line sink rates

TIPPET STRENGTH

Most fly-fishermen identify their leader sizes by X number. The X number is, in effect, an identification by diameter. (Notice that at diameter .011 inches, size OX, the system runs out of X numbers. In diameters from .012 through .020, leaders and tippets are sized 9/5 through 1/5, respectively. In sizes larger than .021 diameter, leaders and tippets are identified by diameter alone.) Lately, though, some manufacturers have been using for their heavier tippets an "aught" system similar to that used for hooks. Above OX the sizes increase from O1X to O2X and so on, as high as you want to go. Most of the time all you need to know is a tippet's diameter (or corresponding size number), but at times it is important to know how strong your tippet is—and that varies considerably. There is on the market a popular little gauge for measuring leader and tippet diameters. The gauge also has a scale, which equates the diameter with X size and test strength. The accuracy of the gauge in estimating breaking strength depends upon the brand of tippet material you are using.

In the table on the next page, I have listed the test strengths on the Gage-It leader gauge, followed by the break loads (or test ratings) of several popular leader and tippet materials. With a few exceptions, I have listed the strength figures as they appear in the

SIZES & STRENGTHS OF FLY-FISHING LEADER & TIPPET MATERIALS

BREAK LOAD IN POUNDS

Diam in	Size	Gage-It Gauge	Aeon	L.L. Bean	Berkley	Sue Burgess	Climax	Cortland	Dai-Riki	Kroic GT	Mason Hard	Maxima	Luxor	Orvis SupStr	Scientific Anglers	Umpqua	Size
.003	8X	0.5	1.3	—	—	—	—	—	—	1.25	—	1	0.75	—	1	—	8X
.004	7X	1	2	—	—	—	2.8	2.4	1.9	1.75	—	1	1.1	2.0	2	2	7X
.005	6X	2	3	3	2	2	3.5	3.2	2.8	2.5	1.0	2	1.4	3.0	3	3	6X
.006	5X	3	4	4	3	3	4.5	4	4	3.25	1.3	3	2.4	4.0	4	4	5X
.007	4X	4	5	5	4	4	6.5	5	5	4.0	2	4	3.1	5.5	5	6	4X
.008	3X	5	6	7	5	6*	8	6.5	7	5.0	2.7	5	3.8	7.0	6	8	3X
.009	2X	6	7	9	6	6–8*	9	9	10	7.25	3.4	6	4.5	9.0	7	10	2X
.010	1X	8	9	11	8	8*	12	11	12	8.25	4	8	5.5	10.0	9	12	1X
.011	0X	9	10	13	10	—	15	13	15	9.75	5	—	6.5	12.0	10	14	0X
.012	9/5	10	—	14	—	—	—	—	—	—	6	10	7.5	13.5	—	—	01X
.013	8/5	12	—	16	12	12	16	15	—	—	7	12	8.6	15.0	—	16	02X
.014	7/5	—	—	18	—	—	—	—	—	—	8	—	—	—	—	—	03X
.015	6/5	15	—	20	15	16	20	18	—	—	10	15	11.6	20.0	—	20	04X
.016	5/5	—	—	—	—	—	—	—	—	—	—	—	—	—	—	25	05X
.017	4/5	20	—	—	—	—	29.5	24	—	—	12	20	15.0	27.0	—	30	06X
.018	3/5	—	—	—	—	—	—	—	—	—	—	—	—	—	—	—	07X
.019	2/5	25	—	—	—	—	35	30	—	—	15	—	—	30.0	—	—	08X
.020	1/5	—	—	—	—	—	—	—	—	—	—	25	—	—	—	—	09X
.021	—	—	—	—	—	—	42	35	—	—	—	—	—	40.0	—	—	010X
.022	—	30	—	—	—	—	—	—	—	—	20	30	—	—	—	—	011X
.023	—	—	—	—	—	—	—	—	—	—	—	—	—	—	—	—	012X
.024	—	40	—	—	—	—	—	—	—	—	—	40	—	—	—	—	013X
.025	—	—	—	—	—	—	—	—	—	—	26	—	—	—	—	—	014X
.028	—	—	—	—	—	—	—	—	—	—	32	—	—	—	—	—	017X
Diam Size		Gauge	Aeon	Bean	Berkley	Burgess	Climax	Cortland	Dai-Riki	Kroic Mason	Maxima	Luxor	SupStr	3M/SA	Umpqua	Size	

NOTE: The Sue Burgess tippet material sizes rated at 6 and 8 pounds are listed in the catalog as 3X and 2X, respectively; but their diameters are listed as .009 and .010 inches, or 2X and 1X.

catalogs of the manufacturers or vendors. For consistency, I have converted fractions to decimals. If whole numbers are listed, they probably represent test ratings; if decimal numbers are listed, they probably represent actual break loads.

Luxor Kroic, the popular French monofilament from Pezon et Michel, is a special problem. Some half dozen or so companies with mail-order catalogs sell Kroic in America. And if you peruse their catalogs, you will see a bewildering array of breaking strengths listed. There are two reasons: (1) At least two forms of Kroic are sold. (2) Because it is made in Europe, Kroic conforms to metric standards, but our X size system is based on inches; the spools are labeled to please the American vendors, without regard to accuracy. Incidentally, the diameters of some of the other brands also fall between the standard diameters listed in the tables. For example, Maxima's finest tippet material measures .0035 inches, midway between 7X and 8X.

Butt   Tapered section   Tippet

Knot   Knot

Knotted or Compound Leader

Butt   Tippet

Knotless Tapered Leader

Tapered leaders

Most of us refer to any leader that gradually reduces in size as a tapered leader. The leaders on the market are identified primarily by tippet size and overall length, although diameter of the leader butt is often listed as well. In commercial parlance, a tapered leader is usually also knotless. What might be called a pre-tied tapered leader is usually called a compound leader.

TIPPET STRENGTH OF COMMERCIAL COMPOUND & TAPERED FLY LEADERS

BREAK LOAD IN POUNDS

Size	Aeon	Dan Bailey Dai-Riki	Dan Bailey Platlon	L.L. Bean	Berkley Specialist	Sue Burgess	Climax	Cortland 333 Pres. I	Hardy Bros.	Orvis Tied	Orvis Knotless	Sci Anglers System	Sci Anglers XHD	Thomas & Thomas	Umpqua	Size
8X	1	—	—	—	—	—	—	—	—	—	—	1	—	—	—	8X
7X	2	1.9	—	—	—	—	2.4	2.4	1.75	1	—	2	—	2.4	—	7X
6X	3	2.8	2.1	3	1.75	2	3.2	3.2	2	1.25	3	3	—	3.2	3	6X
5X	4	4	3.3	4	2	3	4.4	4	2.5	2	4	4	—	4.4	4	5X
4X	5	5	4.3	5	2.5	4	5.5	5	3	3	5	5	—	5.5	5	4X
3X	6	7	5.2	7	3	6	6.5	6.5	3.5	3.5	6	6	—	6.5	7	3X
2X	7	10	6.3	9	4	8	9	9	4	4	7	7	10	9	9	2X
1X	9	12	7.2	11	5	—	11	11	5	5	9	9	12	11	11	1X
0X	10	15	9	13	6	—	13	13	6	6	10	10	15	13	13	0X
9/5	12	—	—	14	—	—	—	—	—	—	12	—	—	—	—	01X
8/5	14	—	—	16	8	—	—	8	—	—	14	—	—	—	—	02X
7/5	15	—	—	18	—	—	—	—	—	—	15	—	—	—	—	03X
6/5	16	—	—	20	10	—	—	10	—	—	16	—	—	—	—	04X
Size	Aeon	Dai-Riki	Platlon	Bean	Berkley	Burgess	Climax	333 Pres. I	Hardy	Orvis		System XHD		T & T	Umpqua	Size

THE RULE OF 11 FOR SIZING LEADERS AND TIPPETS

If you have lost the label that had the diameter of your commercial leader or tippet material printed on it, you can still calculate the diameter (if you remember its X size) by following the **Rule of 11**:

Subtract the X number from 11 to get the diameter:

$$D = 11 - X$$

Example: A 3X tippet would be .008 inches in diameter ($11 - 3 = 8$).

Conversely, if you know or can measure the diameter of your tippet, using calipers, a micrometer, or one of those leader gauges, you can calculate the X size.

Subtract the diameter from 11 to get the X size:

$$X = 11 - D$$

Example: If a piece of leader material measures .009 inches, it could be used to make a 2X tippet ($11 - 9 = 2$).

For tippet sizes larger than OX, you have two options. To use those strange N/5 size numbers, just add 10 to the Rule of 11 and follow the same steps in what I guess we should call the **Rule of 21**:

Subtract the N/5 number from 21 to get the diameter:

$$D = 21 - N$$

Example: If a leader or tippet spool is marked 7/5, you can immediately calculate that its diameter is .014 inches ($21 - 7 = 14$).

Subtract the diameter from 21 to get the N/5 size:

$$N = 21 - D$$

Example: A saltwater tippet of .018 diameter is a 3/5 ($21 - 18 = 3$).

For the new aught-numbering system, use the **Reverse Rule of 11**:

Add 11 to the OX number to get the diameter:

$$D = OX + 11$$

Example: A size O13X tippet would be .024 inches in diameter (13 + 11 = 24).

Subtract 11 from the diameter to get the OX size:

$$OX = D - 11$$

Example: Now a tippet of .018 diameter is an O7X (18 − 11 = 7).

KNOT EFFICIENCY

Many anglers refer to the percentage of unknotted line strength that knots will hold before failing as knot *strength,* but this is not correct. Obviously, lines of lower inherent knot strength will fail sooner, but for the purposes of this table, we will assume that you are using a good premium monofilament that has good knot strength, and that you are tying your knots properly. You shouldn't be using those cheaper, weaker, bargain-basement lines anyway.

The ranges in the ratings below are the result of several things: variations in the test results reported by different laboratories; different inherent knot strengths of the brands of line that were tested; and a slight drop in efficiency when knots are tied in lines of heavier pound-test.

The numbers in the ratings indicate the percentage of the unknotted line's break load (or breaking strength) at which the knots will probably fail, if they were properly tied. Some knots are a lot easier to tie properly than others, the improved clinch being a knot that everyone knows how to tie poorly.

Some knots work better in monofilament than in braided lines (and vice versa), but there doesn't yet exist a good data base of knot efficiencies for braided lines. They should be close enough to the monofilament figures for practical application.

KNOT EFFICIENCIES

Knot	Efficiency (%)
Action Loop Knot (Homer Rhode Loop)	50–75
Albright Knot	95–100
Bimini Twist	100
Blood Knots	
Blood Knot	80–95
Stu Apte-Improved Blood Knot	90–100
Blood Knot Dropper	80–90
Clinch Knots	
Clinch Knot	80–95
Improved Clinch	90–100
Two-Circle Clinch (Trilene Knot)	90–100
Crawford Knot	95
Crimped Sleeve (mono)	95–100
Dropper Loops	
Dropper Loop (Blood Knot Dropper)	80–95
Surgeon's Dropper	90–95
End Loops	
Bimini Twist	100
Homer Rhode (Action) Loop	50–75
Improved End Loop	70–95
Perfection Loop	60–85
Spider Hitch	95–100
Surgeon's Loop	90–95
Uni-knot (Duncan) Loop	90–100
Figure-Eight Knot (mono)	95–100
Homer Rhode Loop Knot (Flemish Loop)	50–75
Hook Snells	
Basic Hook Snell	85–95
Quick Snell (Clinch Snell)	85–95
Tucked Snell	90–95
Uni-Knot Snell (Whipped Snell)	90–95
Jansik Special	90–95
Key Loop	95–100
Lark's Head/Girth Hitch (to hook, swivel)	75–95
Offshore Swivel Knot	90–100
Overhand Knot	40–70
Palomar Knot	95–100
Perfection Loop	60–85
Spider Hitch	95–100
Splices (braided line)	
Line-to-Line Splice	95–100
Spliced Loop	95–100
Square Knot (Reef Knot)	40–70

Knot	Efficiency (%)
Surgeon's Knots	
Surgeon's Knot	90–100
Surgeon's End Loop	90–95
Surgeon's Dropper Loop	90–95
Tucked Sheet Bend	50–75
Turle Knots	
Turle Knot	50–60
Double Turle	60–95
Improved Turle	75–85
Two-Circle Turle	65–85
Uni-Knot System	
Uni-Knot (Duncan Loop)	90–100
Uni-Knot Loop (Duncan Loop)	90–100
Joining Lines (single strands)	85–95
Joining Lines (doubled lines)	95–100
Leader to Line (Offset Uni-knot)	95–100
Shock Leader to Line	95–100
Double-Line "Leader"	90–100
"Wind Knot" (fly-casting knot)	40–60
Wire and Cable Connections	
Big-Game Cable Loop	95–100
Crimped Sleeve	90–100
Figure-Eight Knot	95–100
Haywire Twist	95–100
Heated (Fused) Twist	85–100
Quick-Change Wire Wrap	75–100
Trolling Spoon Loop	90–100

LURE RUNNING DEPTHS

Too few plug manufacturers publish the running depths of their lures. And, since running depth is probably the single most important variable in a lure's performance, that's a shame. (Depth is almost synonymous with water temperature, a key factor in fish movements, and you can't catch fish if your lure is too far above or below them.) At best, most plug makers simply use a descriptive term like "deep runner" to describe a lure's running depth. Each manufacturer may have his own notion as to how deep is "deep," but we're going to hazard some generalities:

Description	Running Depth Range
Surface	At or within 6 inches of the surface
Shallow	From the surface to 1–3 feet
Medium	2 to 4 or 5 feet
Medium-Deep	To 6–8 feet
Deep	To 10–12 feet
Very Deep	To 12–15 feet or more

Further generalities:

Trolling vs. Retrieving Depth: Most plugs will troll deeper than they will run when cast and retrieved.

Cranking Speed: Contrary to popular belief, a slow to medium cranking speed is required to get a diving plug down to its maximum running depth, *not* fast cranking.

Depth Maintenance: A deep-running plug will maintain its depth until it is within 5 to 10 horizontal feet of the rod.

Neutral-buoyancy Lures: Countdown, suspender, or neutral-buoyancy plugs will more or less maintain the depth to which you let them sink. On some such plugs, there is a practical limit beyond which they will not sink, or only sink very slowly; such plugs will not maintain that depth very long when being trolled or retrieved. For the really dense ones, which will hold their maximum depth better, a practical maximum may range from fifteen to twenty-five feet.

Metal Lures: For jigs, spoons, spinners, and the like, they will *start* their trolling or retrieval at the depth to which you let them sink, but few of them will maintain that depth. More typically, the closer they get to the rod, the shallower they run. Also, the faster they are retrieved or trolled, the less deeply they will generally run and the faster they will come up. Hydrodynamics of the metal lure's design plays an important role. For example, the wider a spinner's blade, the shallower it will run.

Some manufacturers do, from time to time, list running depths in their catalogs. The accuracy of such figures is extremely variable, but you can count on their being optimistically deep. From a variety of catalogs and fliers, I have gathered the following running depths for several popular swimming and diving plugs:

Plug	Running Depth
Arbogast	
Arbo-gaster	3–15 feet, cast; 12–20 feet, trolled
Dorado	0–2 ft
Mud-Bug	6½ (¼ oz) to 8 ft (⅝ oz)
Bagley	
Bang-O-Lure	0–1½ ft
Bang-O-Lure Shad	1–6 ft (SF5); to 12 ft (DSF5)
Diving B	To 10 (DB1), 12 (DB2), or 16 ft (DB3)
Kill'r B:	
KB1	To 4 ft
KB2	To 10 ft
DKB1	To 7 ft
DKB2	To 10 ft
DKB3	To 12 ft
Mackeral	To 14 (DB06) or 16 ft (DB08)
Mighty Minnow	0–4 ft (MM); to 7 ft (DMM)
Perch/Walleye	1–6 ft (SF3); to 10 ft (DSF3)
Small Fry series	
SF1	1–4 ft
SF2	0–6 ft
DSF1	To 7 ft
DSF2	To 10 ft
DDSF1	To 10 ft
Small Fry Shad	
SSF3	0–1 ft
SF2	1–4 ft
SF3	1–6 ft
DSF2	To 7 ft
DSF3	To 10 ft
DDSF2	To 10 ft
Bomber	
Baby Bomber 200	4–6 ft
Midget Bomber 300	4–6 ft
Bomber 400	To 7 ft
Bomber 500	To 12 ft
Bomber 600	To more than 15 ft
Model A	8–9 ft (medium); to 10 ft (deep)
Smilin-Minno	3–12 ft
Boone	
Crankster	8 ft (¼ oz) to 9 ft (½ oz)
Buck Perry	
Spoonplug	
100	12–15 ft
200	9–12 ft
250	6–9 ft
400	4–6 ft

Plug	Running Depth
500	2–4 ft
700	15–20 ft
800	20–25 ft

Crankbait
Great Lake Fingerling	5–6 ft, cast; 10–12 ft, trolled
Great Lake Yearling	To 40 ft or more

Creek Chub
Dingbat	0–3 ft
Viper	0–3 ft

Gibbs
Trolling Swimmer	3–4 ft

Heddon
Big Bud	0–4 ft
Devil Diver	15–18 ft
Hedd-Hunter	4–7 ft (med); 8–12 ft (deep)
Hedd-Hunter Minnow	0–2 ft
Hedd-Hunter Popeye	3–6 ft
Lucky 13	2–3 ft
Preyfish	3–5 ft
River Runt	6–8 ft
River Runt Spook	3–6 ft
Tiny River Runt	5–8 ft
Tad-Polly	2–8 ft

Lazy Ike
Lazy Ike	0–1 ft
Natural Ike	6–8 ft (med)

Les Davis
Witch Doctor	To 20 ft

Luhr Jensen
Fishback
20	6–8 ft
40	8–10 ft
60	12–15 ft

Hot Shot
10	8–10 ft
20	To 12 ft, cast; 15–18 ft, trolled
30	6–8 ft, cast; to 10 ft, trolled
50	8–10 ft
70	1–4 ft

Mann
Deep Pig Razorback	To 8 ft

Plug		Running Depth
MirrOlure		
Billfish	BF	4–10 ft (5 in); 8–20 ft (6 in)
Baby Tadpole	BT	2–6 ft
Doodad	DD	0–1 ft
Dynamite	DM	2–6 ft
Little Tom	LT	0–1 ft
Mity Tom	MT	0–½ ft
Shellcracker	SC	2–6 ft
Skipper	SK	0–½ ft
Trailalure	TM	2–10 ft
Teeny Trout	TNT	2–4 ft
Tadpole	TP	3–8 ft
Tom Scat	TS	0–1 ft
Tiny Trout	TT	1–4 ft
Panfish-Master	00	2–8 ft
Spin-It	10	2–6 ft
Spin-Master	14	2–6 ft
Bass-Master	15	3–8 ft
Shiner Minnow	20	3–12 ft
Bass-Master	25	0–½ ft
Pike-Master	30	3–8 ft
	35	0–1 ft
MirrOlure	MM	2–6 ft
	SM	2–6 ft
	XM	2–6 ft
	00M	2–8 ft
	1M	2–6 ft
	2M	3–12 ft
	3M	0–½ ft
	4M	2–4 ft
	6M	1–3 ft
	7M	0–½ ft
	8M	0–1 ft
	9M	2–6 ft
	10M	0–1 ft
	11M	2–6 ft
	13M	1–4 ft
	15M	3–8 ft
	22M	2–4 ft
	23M	0–8 ft
	24M	4–8 ft
	25M	0–½ ft
	27M	4–6 ft
	28M	0–½ ft
	29M	0–4 ft
	30M	3–8 ft

Plug	Running Depth
32M	2–4 ft
33M	2–6 ft
34M	0–½ ft
35M	0–1 ft
37M	4–8 ft
38M	1–4 ft
39M	4–8 ft
42M	2–4 ft
44M	0–1 ft
47M	4–10 ft
51M	1–4 ft
52M	1–4 ft
60M	3–6 ft
65M	10–20 ft
66M	6–12 ft
67M	10–20 ft
68M	4–10 ft
70M	0–1 ft
71M	1–6 ft
72M	2–4 ft
77M	4–8 ft
78M	0–2 ft
79M	2–6 ft
80M	0–1 ft
81M	2–8 ft
82M	1–6 ft
85M	6–12 ft
88M	0–1 ft
91M	0–10 ft
92M	0–14 ft
99M	0–1 ft

Norman

Baby Little N	6–10 ft
Deep Little N	To 20 ft
Deep Runner	To 15 ft (2000); to 30 ft (3000)
Little Scooper	6–10 ft
Magnum Scooper	To 15 ft
Quarter-Back	2–3 ft
Quarter-Back Deep-Runner	8–12 ft
Super Scooper	To 20 ft
Threadfin Shad	6 ft

Rapala

Fat Rap	To 3 ft (shallow); 8–12 ft (deep)
Rapala (sinking)	3–4 ft

Plug	Running Depth
Rebel	
Crawfish	To 5½ ft
Deep Teeny-R	To 10 ft
Smithwick	
Devil's Rooter	Jr.—to 8 ft
	Sr.—to 15 ft
Whopper Stopper	
Crapshooter	5–7 ft
Hellbender	To 25 ft
Baby	To 8 ft
Midget	To 15 ft
Magnum	10–35 ft
Hellcat	½–1 ft
Shadrak	8–10 ft, cast; 12–15 ft, trolled

SWIVELS

Numerous types of swivels—ball-bearing, ball-chain, barrel (both the "Crane" and twisted-eye types), box, machined or big-game (also called offshore or tuna), and pin (for instance, three-way), to name the main types—are available to today's fisherman. All are designed to allow tackle to revolve without twisting the line or leader. And all are what engineers would recognize as thrust bearings. The most important thing about swivels is their **efficiency**—how well, how easily, and how dependably, they swivel. It has been calculated that a top-quality ball-bearing swivel is more than two hundred times more efficient than a good barrel swivel!

Other important swivel attributes include **strength**, both absolute and for its size; **weight** for its size and strength; **size range** that is available; **versatility**—how many of your angling chores can it handle; and **quality consistency**. Here is the way I would rank them:

Swivel Type	Swiveling Efficiency	Size Range	Light Weight	Versatility	Quality Consistency
Ball-Bearing	1	4	4	1	4
Ball-Chain	3	6	2	2	3
Barrel					
"Crane"	4	1	1	3	5
Twisted-Eye	6	3	1	4	6
Box	5	2	5	4	2
Machined	2	5	6	5	1
Pin	7	5	3	5	3

I didn't rate strength, because it is so much a function of size, and because you can judge for yourself in the next table. We should probably note, however, that the machined big-game swivel is much stronger than any other type.

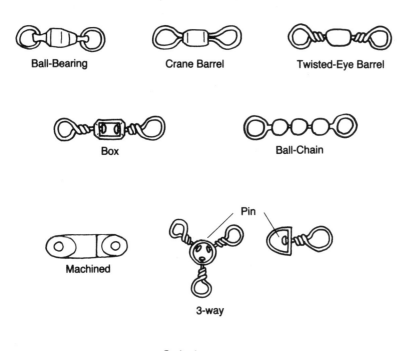

Swivel types

Swivel strength varies from manufacturer to manufacturer, as well as from type to type, and so do the size-numbering systems used. It actually takes three charts to accommodate the nominal size-numbering systems used by the principal swivel manufacturers. Machined big-game swivels and ball-chain swivels are sized by outside diameter, in millimeters (mm). The others use rather arbitrary size numbers—the way hooks do. And, as in the case of hooks, some size numbers get larger as the swivels do, while others run in the opposite direction. Even when the numbers run the same way, it is not safe to assume that the same size numbers are equivalent sizes. Therefore, the following tables should be used as rough guidelines only.

SWIVEL SIZE VS. STRENGTH
TYPICAL BREAKING STRENGTHS (LB)

BARREL AND BOX SWIVELS

Size	"Crane" Barrel	Twisted Barrel	Box	Size	"Crane" Barrel	Twisted Barrel	Box
14	—	7–12	—	1/0	200–214	45–120	104
12	20	10–20	20	2/0	225–295	120	121
11	—	—	22	3/0	300–390	143	141
10	30–75	15–25	24	4/0	350–460	195	163
9	—	25–30	26	5/0	400–490	250	214
8	—	24–36	29	6/0	500–600	—	298
7	35–75	33–42	33	7/0	—	—	408
6	40–75	35–49	37	8/0	900–1000	—	639
5	56–100	40–61	42	9/0	1000	—	728
4	64	45–70	49	10/0	1500	—	—
3	100–101	45–75	60	11/0	1500	—	—
2	125	45–88	73	12/0	1500	—	—
1	150–163	45–100	88				

BALL-BEARING SWIVELS

Size	Split-Ring	Solid Ring
0	—	25
1	10	50
2	12–15	75
3	15–30	100–135
4	30–40	150–175
5	50	200–260
6	60–70	290–300
7	80	310
8	—	500
Size	Split-Ring	Solid Ring

MACHINED (BIG-GAME) AND BALL-CHAIN SWIVELS

Size	Machined	Ball-Chain
2	—	25
3	—	30
4	243	—
5	243	—
6	397	35–45
7	529	—
8	617	—
9	794	—
10	—	75
10.5	992	—
12	1653	—
13	—	120–150
14	1940	—
Size	Big-Game	Ball-Chain

SNAPS

Like swivels, snaps are made in several standard styles (plus a few oddball ones) by a variety of manufacturers, both here and abroad. And, like swivels, the snaps on the market span quite a gamut of quality.

Snap sizes are a little more rational than swivel or hook sizes—at least they all run the same direction—but slight changes in the alloy used, the diameter or temper of the wire, or the precise geometry of its shape can make a big difference in snap performance. A snap's performance can be judged in terms of its **strength**, its **security** against accidental opening, its affect on **lure action** (which is a function both of the shape of the wire's bend and its **weight**), its **convenience** or ease of use, its **versatility**, and its **quality consistency.**

Snap Type	Security	Lure Action	Light Weight	Convenience	Versatility	Consistent Quality
Coastlock	3	4	3	6	4	2
Corkscrew	2	na	5	1	8	3
Cross-Lok	3	4	2	5	2	1
Duo-Lock	4	1	1	3	1	3
Interlock	5	2	2	4	3	4
Lockfast	6	3	4	6	6	6
McMahon	1	4	6	7	7	2
Pompanette	3	4	3	6	4	1
Safety	7	6	2	2	5	5

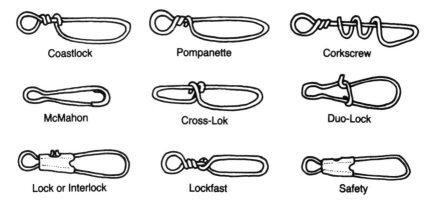

Coastlock   Pompanette   Corkscrew

McMahon   Cross-Lok   Duo-Lock

Lock or Interlock   Lockfast   Safety

Snap types

I downgraded snaps with narrow, asymmetrical shapes for their effect on lure action, and those with hooks and tangs for their inconvenience. Both these features add to security, however.

Once again, I decided not to rank them by strength, because it varies so much with quality and even from maker to maker within the same quality range. Also, size and strength in snaps are even more closely tied than in swivels.

SNAP SIZE VS. STRENGTH

In the chart below, I have combined the test-strength figures I have been able to gather from various manufacturers and catalogs. Let me warn you that sometimes I found different figures for the same snap on different pages of the same manufacturer's catalog. In other words, don't expect these figures to be accurate within plus or minus 10-15 percent, maybe even more. I haven't listed the Lockfast snap because there simply is too much variation in quality. The best ones, made by Bead Chain Tackle Company as an integral part of its rigs, are sized rather oddly but come in three strengths: 25, 75, and 150 pounds. Bead Chain's Interlock snaps, which it calls safety snaps, come in four sizes that test 35, 45, 75, and 120 pounds, but aren't quite equivalent in overall size or wire size to the Interlocks made by other companies.

SNAP STRENGTHS COMPARED BY SIZE & TYPE

		TYPICAL TEST STRENGTH IN POUNDS						
Snap	Size 0	1	2	3	4	5	6	7
Coastlock	—	25	25–30	60–75	90–100	150–165	200–225	300–350
Corkscrew	—	—	—	50	75	165	200	—
Cross-Lok*	—	—	40	75	125	200	300	—
Duo-Lock	—	20	25	40	50	85	150	—
Interlock	—	15	25	30–40	40–50	55–60	60–80	120
McMahon	—	18	40	80	80	100–110	150	—
Pompanette	18	22	50	75	95–100	160–165	200	300
Safety	—	10–15	25	40	50	55	60	75

*NOTE: Berkley, the maker of Cross-Lok snaps, numbers its sizes 1, 3, 6, 9, and 10—perhaps anticipating future sizes—but I have reassigned the numbers to be more nearly equivalent to the others.

EATING THE CATCH

Fortunately for those of us who like to eat at least some of what we catch, most fish are edible. Better than that, they are *good*, being both delicious and nutritious. Some fish are inedible by virtue of their size or boniness, and a few by virtue of their taste. Others have inedible or poisonous parts (shark livers, for instance), and a relative few are generally toxic, at least part of the time in part of their range. Most of us know about the edibility, inedibility, or toxicity of the fish that occur where we live or grew up. And when we travel, we usually have the advice of local experts to fall back upon. But more of us are traveling farther and more often, and being exposed to species that are, to us at least, rather exotic.

In the pages that follow, I have summarized the information I could find on the chemical composition, nutritive value, and toxicity of fish. Naturally, nutritional information is more readily available on species for which a commercial fishery exists. And the results of different researchers can be quite disparate, reflecting differences in research methods as well as considerable variety within a given species according to its size, age, sex, life-cycle stage, and habitat.

HOW FISH RATE, NUTRITIONALLY

Fish have been known as "brain food" for a great many years. Chemists and nutritional scientists have not been able to prove any significant connection between the eating of fish and the development of brain tissue or intelligence. However, eating fish does prove how smart you are, because fish rank among the very best foods, from a nutritional point of view. In most categories, fish range from good to excellent as a source of nutrients.

Chemical Composition

The basic constituents of fish flesh are, in order of their dominance, moisture, protein, fat, ash, and carbohydrates.

Moisture accounts for about 70 to 80 percent of a fish's weight. The moisture includes water, blood, and other body fluids. This certainly improves the palatability of fish, and moisture (water) is an essential part of our diets. But moisture is in virtually everything we eat, and is so easy to come by in our diets that we shouldn't make too much of it here.

Protein is the all-important body builder in our diets. There are actually twenty-two different amino acids included under the name "protein." Thirteen of them are termed "nonessential" because they can be manufactured by the body, but the nine "essential" amino acids must be supplied by our diets. Fortunately, fish is an excellent source of those essential proteins. Some proteins are difficult to digest, but fish proteins are 85 to nearly 100 percent digestible, so are terrific for young children and old people. Most fish flesh contains about 20 percent protein by weight, and a four-ounce serving of fish will supply about half the total amount of protein required by the body each day.

Fat or oil is the great bugaboo in American diets. We simply consume too much of it. No wonder that we have such weight and heart problems. Fish is generally very low in fat content. It is much lower than the cuts of meat we usually eat, and lower even than the leanest and most expensive cuts such as veal. Fish isn't nearly so fattening as other meats, either. Few fish species contribute more than 200 calories per serving, and most will come in closer to 100 calories. Compare that to, say, 300 or so calories for a lean hamburger patty without a bun. Fish are very low in cholesterol, especiallly the low-fat species, and may contain only a tenth the cholesterol found in certain cuts of meat.

Speaking of cholesterol, know that fish fats and oils are rich in unsaturated and polyunsaturated fatty acids. These not only do not contribute to the body's tendency to manufacture cholesterol, they even help the body to suppress cholesterol levels. Ironically, then, the oilier a fish is, the better it tends to be in preventing cholesterol buildup. The species that are especially rich in polyunsaturated fats include pilchards, shad, rainbow trout, Atlantic mackerel, Pacific salmon, albacore, lake whitefish, striped mullet, herrings, swordfish, sea basses, rockfish, and ciscoes.

Cholesterol figures aren't readily available for most fish species, but here are some cholesterol counts I have come across:

Brill	44 mg/100 gm
Carp	75
Catfishes (freshwater)	45
Cod, Atlantic	36
Cod, Pacific	37
Dogfish, Spiny	36
Eel, American	10
Eel, Conger	28
Flying fish	17
Goosefish	35
Grunts	36
Haddock	58
Halfbeaks	200–700
Halibuts	34
Herring, Atlantic	36
Herring, Pacific	195
Jack, Crevalle	138
Jack Mackerel	32
Mackerel, Atlantic	80
Mullet, Striped	21
Pollock	58
Puffer, Northern	113
Porgies	52
Sailfish	6
Sauries	19
Searobins	32
Shark, Blue	5
Shark, Thresher	6 mg/100 gm
Smelt, Pond	72
Snapper, Red	40
Sole, Dover	43
Trout, Rainbow	25–70
Tuna, Bigeye	92
Tuna, Skipjack	18
Tuna, Yellowfin	6
Yellowtail, California	90

Besides the nutritional aspects, the fat or oil content of fish flesh affects its cooking and palatability. Some people like oily fish, others don't. Oily fish generally are better baked or broiled than sauteed or fried. Lean fish can stand the added fat of frying or sauteeing, but they also bake well because they contain more water than do fatty fish. Because cookbooks sometimes specify whether a recipe should use a fatty or nonfatty fish, it helps to know where the dividing lines are:

Very Low Fat Fish	0–2 percent fat content
Low Fat Fish	Less than 5 percent fat
Medium Fat Fish	5 to 15 percent fat
High Fat Fish	More than 15 percent fat

Within a species, there may be a rather considerable range of fat content from fish to fish, and especially from one end of the season to another. Migratory fish tend to store up energy as fat prior to their migrations. Similarly, some fish store fat energy in preparation for spawning.

Another consideration is the location of the fat in the tissue. Generally, flesh near the tail is the least fatty. The closer you get to the head, the fattier the flesh will be. And usually the oiliest flesh is in the belly flaps. This generalization holds truest in reasonably oily fish and applies least well to very lean fish like the cods and crappies.

Ash is an oddball constituent. It is the incombustible part, which includes nonvolatile oxides, salts of metals, nonmetallic atoms like silica, and pure metals. It includes some of the minerals as well as some indigestibles. Because ash content in fish ranges from 0.5 to 1.5 percent, we can afford to ignore it.

Carbohydrates can be murder on a calorie-counting diet, and fish come to the rescue again. Very few fish contain any carbohydrates at all. But watch the way you cook your fish, because breading, battering, or stuffing fish can really add a load of carbohydrates.

Vitamins

Vitamin A is a fat-soluble vitamin. With a few notable exceptions (swordfish, lampreys, eel, whitefish, anchovies, carp, spiny dogfish, gobies, milkfish, sablefish, salmon, sardines, sauries, wolffish, and bigeye tuna) it is not as common in fish flesh as it is in red meat. However, fish liver is an excellent source of vitamin A. Some fish livers, especially shark livers, contain so much vitamin A they are toxic.

B-complex vitamins are water-soluble and are found throughout fish flesh, in about the same amounts as in the meat of land animals. Generally speaking, fish is an excellent source of *biotin, niacin,* and *vitamins B_6* and B_{12}, a good-to-excellent source of *thiamin* and *riboflavin,* and not so good for the other two: *folacin* (folic acid) and *pantothenic acid.* More B vitamins are found in fatty fish than in lean fish, and the dark meat of fish contains many times the B vitamins that are found in light meat.

Vitamin C or ascorbic acid is present in fish, but there are better sources. Ditto for **vitamins E** and **K**.

Vitamin D, like vitamin A a fat-soluble vitamin, is also copiously supplied by fish liver. To a much greater extent than vitamin A, however, vitamin D is also contained in the flesh of fatty fish, some of which are excellent sources of this essential vitamin.

Minerals

Fish are significant sources of several important minerals, among them **iodine, phosphorus, potassium, fluoride, iron, copper, zinc, manganese, cobalt, molybdenum**, and **selenium**. Fish is a particularly good source of potassium and phosphorus. And only marine shellfish top saltwater and anadromous fish as a source of **iodine** in the ordinary diet. **Magnesium** content hasn't been well studied, and varies considerably from species to species and with the habitat, but the available figures suggest that certain fish are excellent sources and most are better sources than meat. As might be expected, red meat contains more **iron** than does fish, but fish is still a very good source. **Calcium** content is higher in fish than in meat, but only those fish that are eaten whole, bones and all (sardines, whitebait, small smelts, and the like), are significant sources of calcium in the diet.

Sodium deserves special consideration. Many people these days have been placed on low-sodium diets, and fresh fish can be important to them. Most low-sodium diets restrict people to 100 milligrams of sodium per 100 grams of food. Most fish do not contain that much sodium. Surprisingly, marine fish are only somewhat higher in sodium content than freshwater fish. Watch

out for canned and processed fish, though, because salt and so-
dium-based preservatives might have been added. In the table
that follows, I have listed all the sodium-content figures I could
find.

The table that follows is based on analyses of 100 grams of
skinned and deboned fish flesh, unless otherwise specified. That is
about three and half ounces, a very small serving in this fish-lov-
ing trencherman's estimation. The figures for protein, fat, and
carbohydrates are for grams per 100 grams of flesh; this means the
figures are also percentages. The figures for sodium are listed in
milligrams per 100 grams. And calories are just calories.

A variety of sources was used, and fairly wide ranges exist for
some of the entries. Most of the time this reflects differences with
season, size, and maturity of the fish, as well as differences in
environmental factors that may affect a fish's condition. Sometimes, though, the range reflects different analytical methods used
by various researchers.

COMPOSITION AND NUTRITIONAL VALUES OF VARIOUS FISHES (100 grams of Raw Flesh)

Fish	Protein gm	Fat gm	Sodium mg	Calories cal	This Species Is a Better Source than Most Fish for These Important Minerals; Vitamins; Polyunsaturated Fatty Acids (PFA)
Albacore	13–28	1–18	51	107–185	Potassium, Phosphorus; Niacin; PFA
Alewife	12–20	3–15	110	132	Potassium, Phosphorus; Riboflavin, B_{12}
Amberjack, Greater	15–23	1–21	52–90	96–154	Thiamin, B_{12}
Anchovy, Northern	11–17	4–27	—	160	—
Anchovy, Striped	16–19	1.6–4.6	—	94	—
Anchovies	11–22	0.5–3.8	148	73–103	Potassium, Iron, Zinc, Iodine; Riboflavin, Folacin, A, B_{12}
Angelfish, Queen	20	0.2	—	83	—
Barracuda, Great	18–22	0.2–10	46–154	77–110	Phosphorus, Iron; Niacin
Barracuda, Pacific	21	2.5	132	97	Phosphorus, Iron
Bass, Bank Sea	17	1.5	—	72	—
Bass, Black Sea	18–19	1–3	68	89	—
Bass, Giant Sea	18	0.1	—	73	Thiamin
Bass, Kelp	20	0.1	—	81	—
Bass, Rock	19	0.9	—	84	—
Bass, Striped	16–19	1.5–2.9	—	90–150	—
Bass, White	18	3	—	92	—
Basses, Sea	15–21	0.4–3.7	44–90	90	—
Blennies, Combtooth	18–21	2.4	—	81–113	—
Bloater	19	14	—	202	—

Fish	Protein gm	Fat gm	Sodium mg	Calories cal	This Species Is a Better Source than Most Fish for These Important Minerals; Vitamins; Polyunsaturated Fatty Acids (PFA)
Bluefish	20–22	2.1–4.8	60–74	196	Phosphorus, Iron, Magnesium; Thiamin, Niacin
Bluegill	13	2.3	—	78	Calcium, Iron, Zinc
Bocaccio	19	1.5	60	89	Potassium
Bonito, Atlantic	19–29	2–12	—	142	Phosphorus, Iron
Bonito, Pacific	23	3–10	—	159	Phosphorus, Iron; Riboflavin, Niacin
Bowfin	20	1.4	—	90	—
Brill	18	0.1–5	94	92	Phosphorus
Buffalo, Bigmouth	15	17	—	210	—
Bullhead, Black	16	2	—	80	—
Bumper, Atlantic	18	0–11	—	120	—
Burbot	17–19	0.6–1.2	—	78	Iodine; Thiamin, Riboflavin
Butterfish	16–18	5–17	81	114–169	Potassium
Capelin	15	3	—	88	—
Carp, Common	12–21	1–15	48–80	115–125	Phosphorus; Thiamin, Riboflavin, A, B_{12}
Catfish, Channel	16–21	1–11	—	119	Zinc; Thiamin, Niacin
Catfish, Hardhead	16	4–9	98–103	120	Phosphorus
Catfishes, freshwater	15–23	0.3–21	60	103–157	Potassium, Calcium, Magnesium; Thiamin, A, B_{12}
Chilipepper	21	2–6.3	55	102–105	—
Chubs, Sea	19	1.2	50	86	—
Cisco	16–21	1.5–7.2	38–56	106	PFA
Cisco, Longjaw	12–17	7.6–21.5	—	154	—
Cisco, Shortjaw	18	9	—	152	—
Cisco, Shortnose	16	13	—	180	—
Cobia	19	4–10	—	124	—
Cod, Atlantic	15–21	0.1–0.8	49–92	73–78	Potassium, Phosphorus, Magnesium, Iron, Zinc; Thiamin, Riboflavin, A
Cod, Pacific	15–19	0.1–2	71–76	70	Potassium, Phosphorus
Crappie, White	17	0.8	—	74–79	—
Croaker, Atlantic	14–19	0.4–3	87	90–96	Potassium, Phosphorus, Iron, Zinc; Thiamin, Riboflavin

Fish	Protein gm	Fat gm	Sodium mg	Calories cal	This Species Is a Better Source than Most Fish for These Important Minerals; Vitamins; Polyunsaturated Fatty Acids (PFA)
Cusk	17–20	0.2–1.8	—	79	Iron, Zinc, Iodine
Dabs	12–18	0.4–3	—	84–91	Iron, Zinc
Dogfish, Smooth	26	0.2	100	106	Phosphorus, Iron; Niacin
Dogfish, Spiny	16–20	5–15	100	156	Phosphorus; Riboflavin, Niacin, A
Dolly Varden	20	6.5	—	134	—
Dolphin	19	0.2–3.2	98–242	94	Potassium, Iron; Riboflavin, A
Dories	16–21	0.5–6.3	60	80–104	Potassium
Drum, Black	18	0.5	51	78	—
Drum, Freshwater	16–18	1–8.4	70–73	119–121	Potassium; Riboflavin, Niacin, B_{12}
Drum, Red	19	1	55	85	—
Drum, Sand	15–16	4	—	98	—
Eel, American	16–18	12–22	30–81	199–255	Phosphorus, Zinc; Riboflavin, A, B_{12}
Eel, Conger	16–19	4.5–12	50–89	111–178	Iron, Zinc, Iodine; Niacin, A, B_{12}
Eulachon	15	6.5	—	117	—
Filefishes	19	0.3	—	81	Potassium
Flounder, Arrowtooth	16	2–9	59	108	Potassium, Magnesium, Iron
Flounder, Gulf	20	0.8	54–160	88	—
Flounder, Southern	17–19	0.8–1.2	54	79–86	Thiamin, Niacin
Flounder, Starry	17–18	1–4	85–99	85	Potassium, Phosphorus; Thiamin, Riboflavin, Niacin
Flounder, Summer	20	0.1–1	78	84	—
Flounder, Winter	14–22	0.2–3	35–99	77	Thiamin, Riboflavin, Niacin
Flounder, Witch	16	0.1–1	35–99	77	Iron, Zinc
Flounder, Yellowtail	18–22	0.3	33–79	87	Potassium; Thiamin, Niacin
Flyingfishes	17–24	0.2–1.4	70–112	88–100	Phosphorus
Goatfishes	18–23	1–7	40–98	99–120	Potassium, Calcium, Iron
Gobies	14–21	0.1–5.2	50–150	74–103	Potassium, Phosphorus, Iron; A
Goldfish	15–18	0.3–7.5	—	99	Iron, Zinc; A
Goosefishes	11–23	0.3–2.5	180	58–95	Niacin

Fish	Protein gm	Fat gm	Sodium mg	Calories cal	This Species Is a Better Source than Most Fish for These Important Minerals; Vitamins; Polyunsaturated Fatty Acids (PFA)
Grouper, Black	20	0.7	—	88	—
Grouper, Red	20	0.2–4	80	90	Riboflavin
Groupers	16–21	0.2–2.3	—	83–94	—
Grunt, Bluestriped	21	0.6	—	90	Calcium, Iron
Grunt, White	20	0.2	—	80	Niacin
Grunts	16–21	0.2–2.7	70–72	80–93	Thiamin, Riboflavin, Niacin, A
Guaguanche	21	0.5	—	87	—
Haddock	15–20	0.1–1.2	54–57	77–79	Potassium, Phosphorus, Iron, Zinc, Iodine; Riboflavin
Hake, Pacific	17	1.7–2.6	111–140	82	Potassium, Magnesium; Riboflavin, Niacin, Folacin, B$_{12}$
Hake, Red	16	0.5	92	70	Potassium
Hake, Silver	15–17	0.2–2	74–95	73–111	Potassium
Hake, Spotted	13	0.8	—	58	—
Halfbeaks	20	0.9	65–81	91	Potassium, Iron
Halibut, Atlantic	12–20	0.7–5.2	49–112	98–126	Riboflavin, Niacin, A, B$_{12}$
Halibut, Pacific	15–24	0.4–6	59	91	Potassium; Thiamin, Niacin
Halibuts	15–24	0.4–13.2	36–112	119	Potassium, Magnesium; Thiamin, Riboflavin, A
Hammerheads	21–23	0.3	—	88–97	Niacin
Harvestfish	16	4.4	—	104	—
Herring, Atlantic	15–22	2–29	52–160	160–176	Iron, Zinc, Iodine; Thiamin, Riboflavin, Niacin, A, B$_{12}$; PFA
Herring, Pacific	9.4–25	3–13	74–160	150	Potassium, Magnesium, Iron; Riboflavin, B$_{12}$; PFA
Herring, Skipjack	20	3	122	122	PFA
Houndfish	21–27	0.8	—	108	Iron
Inconnu	20	6–8	—	141	—
Jack, Crevalle	19	2	—	94	—
Jack, Spotted (Omilu)	21	1.6	—	99	—
Jack Mackerel	18–21	0.2–15	89–94	102	Iron; Niacin
Jacks	17–22	0.1–6.1	54–89	84–135	Iron, Zinc; Niacin, B$_{12}$
Kingfish, Northern	17–18	1–6	83	92–105	—
Kingfish, Southern	18	1–5	83–87	101	—

Fish	Protein gm	Fat gm	Sodium mg	Calories cal	This Species Is a Better Source than Most Fish for These Important Minerals; Vitamins; Polyunsaturated Fatty Acids (PFA)
Ladyfish	19	0.3	—	80	—
Lampreys	13–21	13–19	—	204	Thiamin, Riboflavin, Niacin, A
Leatherjacket	19–21	0.1–1.8	—	88–130	—
Lingcod	17–19	0.5–1	54–62	81–117	Potassium, Magnesium, Iron; Thiamin, Riboflavin, Niacin, B$_{12}$; Insulin
Lizardfishes	17–24	0.1–3.4	70	86–121	—
Lookdown	21	1.8	—	99	Iron; Thiamin, Niacin, B$_{12}$
Lumpfish	6–9	4–8	275	84	—
Mackerel, Atka	18	3–19	—	138	—
Mackerel, Atlantic	15–24	0.7–24	48	84–230	Phosphorus, Magnesium, Iron, Zinc; Riboflavin, Niacin, A, B$_{12}$; PFA
Mackerel, Chub	16–25	0–16	99	142	Potassium, Phosphorus, Iron; Riboflavin, Niacin, B$_{12}$
Mackerel, Frigate	19–26	0.7–7.2	252	120	Potassium, Phosphorus, Iron; Thiamin, Riboflavin, Niacin
Mackerel, King	23	4.6	—	133	Niacin
Mackerel, Spanish	18–22	1–14	68–89	132–177	Calcium, Potassium, Iron, Zinc; Riboflavin, Niacin, B$_{12}$
Marlin, Black	23	0.6	71	96	Zinc
Marlin, Blue	23	3	71	121	—
Marlin, Striped	21	0.3–5	71	109	—
Milkfish	20	4–6	72	132	Iron; Niacin, Folacin, A, B$_{12}$
Minnows	16	1	—	75	—
Moonfish, Pacific	24	2	73	117	—
Morays	20	4	25	116	Potassium; Riboflavin, Niacin
Mu (Levovangan)	17–20	0.6–1.8	93–161	88	—
Mullet, Striped	16–23	0.2–20	58–100	102–219	Potassium, Magnesium, Iron, Zinc, Iodine; Thiamin, Riboflavin, Niacin, Folacin; PFA
Muskellunge	20	3	—	103	Iron
Needlefishes	17–27	0.3–2.1	79	78–121	Magnesium
Parrotfishes	19–21	0.4–2	103	104	Potassium
Perch, Ocean	17–24	0.6–8	59–111	102	Calcium, Potassium, Iron, Zinc, Iodine; B$_{12}$
Perch, Pacific Ocean	17–19	1.2–1.5	62–79	91	Potassium

Fish	Protein gm	Fat gm	Sodium mg	Calories cal	This Species Is a Better Source than Most Fish for These Important Minerals; Vitamins; Polyunsaturated Fatty Acids (PFA)
Perch, Silver (whole)	17	3	—	96	—
Perch, White	19	4	—	118	—
Perch, Yellow	17–20	0.5–4	67–68	85–91	Iron, Zinc; Thiamin, Riboflavin, Niacin
Pigfish (whole)	17	5	—	92	—
Pike, Northern	19	1	29–52	93	Calcium, Potassium, Iron, Zinc; Thiamin
Pilchards (whole)	15–19	0.3–21.4	—	70–285	PFA
Plaice, American	17	0–2	83–98	82	—
Pollock	17–24	0–2	34–86	84	Thiamin, Niacin, B_{12}
Pollock, Walleye	17–18	1	—	74	Potassium, Phosphorus; B_{12}
Pomfret, Atlantic	20	1	—	86	—
Pompano, African	18	0.9	—	88	—
Pompano, Pacific	19	1–3	120	100	Phosphorus, Iron; Niacin
Pompanos	18–21	0.2–8	—	83–115	Iron; Thiamin, Riboflavin, Niacin
Porgy, Longspine	17	2	—	92	—
Porgy, Red	20	1.5	—	95	B_{12}
Puffer, Northern	19	0.4	—	78	—
Rabbitfishes	21	0.7	66–76	90	Potassium
Redhorses	18	1.3	—	102	—
Rockfishes	13–21	0.2–3.5	45–94	76–90	Niacin, B_{12}
Runner, Blue	21	1–3	—	96	—
Runner, Rainbow	22	0.6–3	54	100	Potassium, Iron; Niacin
Sablefish	13–14	13–15	56	188	Potassium, Magnesium, Iron, Iodine; A
Sailfish	16–24	1–4	71	101	—
Salmon, Atlantic	12–23	0.2–15	—	125	Magnesium, Iron, Zinc; Niacin; PFA
Salmon, Chinook	13–26	2.2–19	38–65	182	Magnesium, Iron, Zinc; Riboflavin, Niacin, A; PFA
Salmon, Chum	18–26	1–8	50	123	Potassium, Magnesium, Iron, Zinc; A; PFA
Salmon, Coho	21–22	1–10	26–51	136	Magnesium, Iron; Niacin, A; PFA
Salmon, Pink	17–22	1–8	56–110	124	Potassium, Iron; Niacin; PFA
Salmon, Sockeye	14–23	2–13	48	143	Potassium, Iron, Zinc; Niacin, Folacin, A; PFA

Fish	Protein gm	Fat gm	Sodium mg	Calories cal	This Species Is a Better Source than Most Fish for These Important Minerals; Vitamins; Polyunsaturated Fatty Acids (PFA)
Sand Lances	18–19	0.3–1.5	—	87–91	Zinc; Riboflavin, Niacin, Folacin, B_{12}; PFA
Sardines	17–22	2–27	60–128	139–248	Iron, Zinc; Niacin, A; PFA
Sauries	13–24	1–21	60	121–182	Magnesium, Iron; Niacin, A, B_{12}
Sawfishes	22	5	—	128	Niacin
Scad, Bigeye	20	0–3	61	88	Potassium, Phosphorus, Iron; Niacin, B_{12}
Scad, Mackerel	22	2–4	53–94	99	—
Scup	18–19	1–6	63	102–112	—
Searobins	17–23	1–3	—	98	Magnesium
Seatrouts	17	1–11	54–60	88–121	Zinc; Niacin, A, B_{12}
Shad, American	16–20	1.7–17	54	170–173	Iron; Thiamin, Niacin; PFA
Shad, Hickory	19	5	—	117	Phosphorus; PFA
Shark, Angel (fin)	28	0.4	—	114	—
Shark, Horn	18	0.3	—	76	—
Shark, Salmon	13–21	0.2–24	—	178	—
Shark, Sevengill	15	13	—	189	Zinc
Shark, Soupfin	19	1	—	91	—
Shark, Soupfin (fin)	25	0.4	—	103	—
Shark, Thresher	20	0.3–3.3	—	93	—
Shark, Thresher (fin)	25	0.1	—	99	—
Sharks, Requiem (Gray)	11–25	0.2–3.5	—	72–120	Magnesium, Iron, Zinc; Niacin
Silversides	20	1–2	—	91	Niacin
Skate, Thornback	21	0.2	104	85	Zinc
Skates	13–26	0.2–6.1	90–105	93	Magnesium, Zinc
Smelt, Pond	17	2.9	—	95	Iron; Riboflavin
Smelt, Rainbow	19	2	—	93	Zinc
Smelts	14–19	1–7	80–214	86	Iron, Zinc; B_{12}

Fish	Protein gm	Fat gm	Sodium mg	Calories cal	This Species Is a Better Source than Most Fish for These Important Minerals; Vitamins; Polyunsaturated Fatty Acids (PFA)
Snapper, Colorado	18–21	1.3	—	91	Niacin
Snapper, Gray	18	1.6	—	90	Thiamin
Snapper, Green (Filoa)	20	1.4	61	94	—
Snapper, Red	20	0.4–7.4	63–150	104	Potassium, Iron; Thiamin
Snapper, Yellowtail	20	0.8	—	87	—
Snappers	17–22	0.4–7.4	33–150	82–146	Potassium, Iron; Niacin
Snook	14–21	0.3–1.9	66–80	79–86	Magnesium, Iron; Riboflavin, Niacin
Sole, Dover	14–17	0.4–1.2	95	78	Thiamin, Niacin
Sole, English	15–19	1–2	85	82	Potassium; Niacin
Sole, Petrale	15–20	1–7	81	85–92	Niacin
Sole, Rex	14–19	0.7	150	72	Niacin
Sole, Rock	19	1.2	80	85	Potassium
Sole, Sand	17	0.5	56	73	—
Sole, Yellowfin	17	1.1	—	80	—
Spadefish	15–21	1–7	94	102	Iron; Riboflavin, Niacin, B_{12}
Spot	18–19	2.9–15.9	61	100–219	Riboflavin
Squawfish, Northern	16–18	1.8–3.1	—	96	—
Squawfish, Sacramento	17	2.5	—	91	—
Stingrays	16–25	0.2–0.6	133–179	86	Magnesium, Iron; Niacin, B_{12}
Sturgeon, Lake	17	9.1	—	158	—
Sturgeons (avg.)	18	1.9	—	90–94	Magnesium, Iron
Sucker, White	18	1–2	—	84	—
Suckers	18–21	1–8	50–59	102–104	—
Sunfish	20	1–2	—	97	Iron
Swordfish	17–21	2–7	102	87–118	Phosphorus; Niacin, Folacin, A, B_{12}; PFA
Tautog	18–19	0.2–1.1	50	75–89	—
Tench	17	0.4–1.7	—	84	Magnesium, Iron

Fish	Protein gm	Fat gm	Sodium mg	Calories cal	This Species Is a Better Source than Most Fish for These Important Minerals; Vitamins; Polyunsaturated Fatty Acids (PFA)
Thornyhead, Shortspine	17	1.7	77	85	—
Threadfin, Atlantic	18	2–11	60–96	114	—
Tilefish	19	0.5–1.8	—	85	Iron, Iodine; Riboflavin, Niacin
Tomcod	17	0.4	—	72	—
Trevally, Giant	20–22	0.9–5.6	—	114	Iron; Niacin, A, B_{12}
Triggerfishes	18	0.8	30–70	81	Iron, Zinc
Tripletail	20	0.7	—	88	Iron
Trout, Brook	14–21	3.4–5.5	—	96	—
Trout, Brown	19	2–3	—	100	Iron, Zinc; Riboflavin
Trout, Lake	16–20	7–22	24–54	169	Iron, Zinc; Niacin
Trout, Lake (Siscowet)	8–13	33–67	24–54	491	Iron, Zinc; Niacin
Trout, Rainbow	18–22	2–14	52	154	Potassium, Iron, Zinc; Thiamin, Riboflavin, Niacin, B_{12}; PFA
Tuna, Bigeye	16–27	0.6–3.5	—	110–116	Magnesium, Iron; Thiamin, Niacin, A, B_{12}
Tuna, Bluefin	20–27	0.2–8	39–100	114–171	Iron; PFA
Tuna, Skipjack	21–27	0.2–11	25–52	141	Potassium, Phosphorus, Magnesium, Iron; Thiamin, Niacin, Folacin, B_{12}, C
Tuna, Yellowfin	22–26	0.1–12	37–489	114–131	Iron, Iodine; Thiamin, Niacin, B_{12}
Tunny, Little	22–25	0.7–20	—	134	Potassium, Iron
Turbot, Greenland	17	3.5	—	99	Iron
Turbots	12–18	1–16	68	99–149	Magnesium, Iron
Ulua, Pake	19–22	0.4–6.3	—	105	—
Wahoo	23	1–2	—	105	—
Walleye	19–20	0.5–1.9	52	90	—
Weakfish	16–20	1.4–4.3	59	94	Thiamin, Niacin
Whitefish, Lake	15–20	1.7–18.5	52	140	Zinc; Niacin; PFA
Wolffish, Atlantic	18	2–3	76	96	Zinc, Iodine; A
Wreckfish	17	1–7	119	107	Magnesium, Iron, Zinc
Yellowtail, California	19–23	1–4	75–90	100	Iron; Niacin, B_{12}

COMPOSITION OF RAW ROE OF VARIOUS FISHES

Type	Protein gm	Fat gm	Carbohydrate gm	Calories
Bass, Black Sea	17	4	1.2	107
Bonito, Pacific	17	3	3	107
Cod, Atlantic	24	2.3	1.5	130
Cod, Pacific	21	2	1.3	104
Dogfish, Spiny	25	24	1.4	324
Herring, Pacific	17	0.5–2.7	1.7	90
Herrings	15–25	2–7	2.7	127
Lumpfish	14	3.6	2.4	96
Mackerel, Chub	23	5	3	151
Pollock, Walleye	25	2	2	127
Salmon, Chum	18	10–17	10.1	226
Salmon, Coho	9–28	11	11.1	219
Salmon, Sockeye (salted)	25	15	0.8	236
Searobin	16	7	1.2	134
Shad	23	4	0	128
Sturgeon	26	15–24	0	279
Trout, Rainbow	19	4–15	0	159

NOTE: All fish roes tend to be richer than fish flesh in carbohydrates, vitamins, minerals, and, unfortunately, cholesterol. For example, 100 grams (3½ ounces) of searobin fillets contains approximately 32 milligrams of cholesterol. The same size serving of searobin roe would contain about 252 milligrams of cholesterol. Salmon roe varies in cholesterol levels, from 290 to 580 milligrams per 100 gram serving: Chinook, 580 mg; Chum, 400 mg; Pink, 290 mg; Sockeye, 390 mg.

EDIBLE YIELDS

Whether for nutritional or other reasons, a fisherman often wants to know before he quits fishing just how much edible fish he has. As you know from your own experience, the edible yield varies considerably from species to species, and from fish to fish within a species. Unfortunately, not many fishermen keep and publish their edible-yield statistics, such information apparently doesn't concern ichthyologists and fishery biologists, and nutritionists and food scientists haven't done much work in this area. There are, however, some rough guidelines or rules of thumb.

PORTION-PLANNING GUIDELINES

As I mentioned earlier, nutritionists—purely for the sake of mathematical convenience—deal in 100-gram servings. That's only 3½ ounces of fish, about half a serving, the way I eat fish. More reasonable, if less scientific, is this old-fashioned rule:

One serving = 12 oz. of whole, undressed fish
8 oz. of pan-dressed fish
7 oz. of fish steaks
6 oz. of fillets or chunks
3 oz. of canned fish

And how much edible fish is that? More guidelines:

EDIBLE-YIELD GUIDELINES

Again, the actual edible yield varies from fish to fish, depending upon a lot of things: skeletal structure, skin thickness, fin size, general body shape, the general ease of cleaning, and so on. But there are some generally useful rules:

100% from Fillets and Boneless Chunks
80–85% from Steaks
67% from Pan-dressed Fish
45% from Whole, Undressed Fish

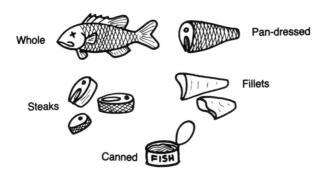

Forms of fish

All right, then, if you weigh your fish when you catch it, you can figure on slightly less than half of it turning into meat in your belly. The actual edible yield of flesh from a whole fish may vary considerably, from as little as 20 percent of the round, undressed weight to as much as 67 percent. Swim bladders take up a lot of gut space, but weigh almost nothing; some fish don't have such bladders but may, like sharks, have huge, heavy, and inedible livers. Others, like amberjacks, have enormous guts for their size, guts that may be stuffed with things they ate but you shouldn't. Still others, like searobins and sculpins, seem to be all head and no body. And then there are those with big, heavy, complicated skeletons or thick, unpalatable skin.

In the table that follows, I have listed the edible-yield figures I have been able to find. Remember, the yield figures are for the form that will go on the plate. You can eat all the fillet yield, about 80 percent of the steak yield, and only about two-thirds of the pan-dressed yield. In the case of sharks, the steak yield is expressed as skinless steaks. Since sharks have no bones and only a rudimentary cartilaginous skeleton, the actual edible yield from skinless shark steak is closer to 90 percent. The edible yield from other fish steaks depends mostly on whether you eat the skin and any fatty flesh that may lie just under the skin. And if the fish you catch is particularly fat or skinny, its edible yield may differ rather considerably from the figures listed below or the ones calculated from the guidelines listed above.

Fish	Fillet	Yield in Other Form
Albacore	60%	
Amberjack	33	
Anchovy	50	
Bass, Striped	40	65% as Steaks
Bonito	50	
Buffalo	25	
Cabezon	20	
Carp	25	
Catfish, Channel	50	
Cod, Pacific	40	
Corbina, California	33	
Dolphin	25	
Dory	25	
Drum, Red	33	
Eel, American		70%, Pan-dressed
Flounder, Starry	40	
Flounder, Summer	50	
Flounder, Winter	40	
Goosefish, tail portion only	50–60	
Groupers	30–40	(Depends on size of fish)

Fish	Fillet	Yield in Other Form
Halibut, California	65%	
Halibut, Pacific	50–65	
Herring, Atlantic or Pacific	50	
Jack Mackerel	50	
Jacksmelt		80%, Pan-dressed
Lingcod	40	
Mackerel, Chub	50	
Pompano, Pacific		60–70%, Pan-dressed
Rockfish	30–40	
Sablefish	40	
Salmon	50–67	
Sanddab		50%, Pan-dressed
Seabass, White	40	65% as Steaks
Seatrout	33	
Shark, Leopard	20	20% as Skinless Steaks
Shark, Thresher	20	20% as Skinless Steaks
Skates, wings only	50	
Snapper, Red	33	
Sole, English	20–30	
Sole, Petrale	35	
Sole, Rex	35	
Sturgeon, White		50% as Steaks
Tilefish	40	
Trout (wild)	33–60	
Trout, Rainbow (farmed)	67	
Wahoo	60	
Yellowtail, California	60	

TOXIC WHEN EATEN

Toxic fish can first be broken into three categories: fish that are always toxic, those that are occasionally toxic, and those that become toxic because of decomposition. Within each category there are several types of toxins. Fortunately, some of these poisons are restricted to the tropical Indo-Pacific (which usually includes Hawaiian waters), but our subtropical Atlantic waters can produce plenty of poisonous fish, and some fish poisons can be found almost anywhere. The lists that follow, although by no means complete, cover many of the ichthyotoxins most likely to be encountered by North American and Hawaiian anglers.

FISH THAT ARE ALWAYS TOXIC

Toxic Skin and Skin Slime (Ichthyocrinotoxic Fish)

These fish may be eaten, so long as they are skinned first, and none of the slime, foam, or mucus on the skin is allowed to contaminate the flesh. The mucus can be removed with a concentrated brine solution. But care must be taken not to get this toxic slime on your skin, **and especially not in your eyes**.

Symptoms of ichthyocrinotoxic poisoning may include nausea and vomiting; diarrhea and abdominal pain; weakness; skin irritation; severe irritation to the eyes. Symptoms usually occur within a few hours and last several days.

Suspect fish include:

Puffers (Tetraodontidae, Canthigasteridae)
Filefishes (Alutoridae)
Triggerfishes (Balistidae)
Porcupine Fishes (Diodontidae)
Trunkfishes (Ostraciidae), also called Boxfishes or Cow Fishes
Soapfishes (Serranidae)
Toadfishes (Batrachoididae)
Hagfishes (Myxinidae)
Lampreys (Petromyzontidae)
Morays (Muraenidae)

Puffer Poisoning (Tetraodontoxic Fish)

In some few species of puffers the flesh itself is poisonous, but usually only if it has been contaminated during cleaning by contact with the generally toxic parts: liver, gonads, roe, intestines, visceral fluid.

Symptoms of this extremely violent but variable toxin include a tingling sensation in the lips and tongue, sometimes spreading throughout the body; floating sensation; loss of motor coordination; salivation; weakness; nausea and vomiting; diarrhea and abdominal pain; muscular twitching, paralysis, and convulsions; lowered body temperature; respiratory paralysis and death (60 percent mortality rate). Symptoms usually begin in ten to forty-five minutes.

Suspect fish include:

Puffers (Tetraodontidae, Canthigasteridae) 80 spp.
Porcupine Fishes (Diodontidae)
Ocean Sunfishes or Molas (Molidae)

Toxic Gonads and Roe (Ichthyootoxic Fish)

This ichthyotoxin seems to be most prevalent among fish taken from fresh and brackish waters in Europe and Asia, but it can be found in certain fish taken in our waters. The flesh may still be edible. In the case of sturgeon roe, only a few cases are on record involving one of the European sturgeons, and those cases are suspect. Obviously, sturgeon roe, when salted and preserved as caviar, is perfectly safe.

Symptoms usually develop within an hour and last for about five days; they may include nausea and vomiting; diarrhea and abdominal pain; cold sweats; chest pain; fever; dizziness; headache; thirst, a dry mouth, or a bitter taste in the mouth; pupillary dilatation; pallor; rapid, irregular, and weak pulse; low blood pressure; muscular cramps; paralysis; convulsions; death (infrequently).

Suspect fish include:

Gars (Lepisosteidae), esp. Alligator Gar (*Lepisosteus spatula*)
Salmons (Salmonidae)
Pikes (Esocidae)
Minnows and Carps (Cyprinidae)
Catfishes (Siluroidei)
Killifishes and Tooth Carps (Cyprinodontidae), esp. the
　　European Barbel (*Barbus meridionalis*)
Burbot (*Lota lota*)
Sculpins (Cottidae), including Cabezon (*Scorpaenichthys
　　marmoratus*)
Certain perchlike fish (Percoidei)
Ratfishes or Chimaeras (Chimaeridae)
Sea Urchins (Echinoidea) during spawning
Sturgeons (Acipenseridae)

Vitamin A Poisoning (Hypervitaminosis A)

Shark liver is the usual source of vitamin A poisoning, but hypervitaminosis A may also be caused by eating the liver or viscera of certain skates and rays, and may be involved in fish-liver poisoning described below. Many of these species are otherwise quite edible.

Symptoms, which may develop within thirty minutes, include nausea and vomiting; diarrhea and abdominal pain; headache; rapid, weak pulse; a burning sensation in the throat and tongue; muscular cramps; visual disturbances; tingling fingertips; joint aches; delirium; respiratory distress; coma; death (relatively high mortality rate).

Suspect fish include:

> Many sharks, particularly tropical, subtropical, and warm-temperate species
> Some skates and rays (Rajiformes)

Fish-Liver Poisoning (Ichthyohepatotoxic Poisoning)

This toxin may be partly due to hypervitaminosis A, but fish other than sharks may be involved. Except for their livers, these fish may otherwise be edible. For some species, the toxicity appears to be seasonal in nature.

Symptoms appear within an hour, usually reach maximum severity in about seven hours, and may last several days. They include nausea and vomiting; fever; severe headache; skin rash and flushed face; rapid pulse; sloughing of skin after several days.

Suspect fish include:

> Sharks, Skates, and Rays (Chondrichthyes)
> Several perchlike fish of the order Perciformes,
> esp. Japanese species
> Giant Sea Bass (*Stereolepis gigas*) seasonally

Poisonous Sharks

I'm not sure what toxin may be involved, but two sharks should not be eaten at all. They are the Greenland shark (*Somniosus microcephalus*) of the cold waters of the North Atlantic and the swell shark (*Cephaloscyllium ventriosum*) that is sometimes caught below Monterey, California. Their flesh is poisonous when eaten. Even a small quantity of swell shark flesh will cause nausea and diarrhea. Greenland shark may be eaten when its flesh has been dried or leached, but otherwise it causes symptoms that resemble those of drunkenness. Whether the closely related Pacific sleeper sharks of the genus *Somniosus* are also toxic, I do not know. It probably is best to avoid them.

FISH THAT MAY BE TOXIC OCCASIONALLY

Ciguatera

Ciguatera is caused by a toxin produced by a type of algae associated with damaged coral reefs. Cigautoxin is usually associated with tropical marine reef fish, particularly those that occur around Caribbean and Indo-Pacific islands; it does not occur in freshwater fish. Plankton-feeding fish also seem to be exempt. Ciguatera's occurrence may be extremely localized, affecting fish only on one side of an island. Ciguatoxin is cumulative, so the older and larger a fish is, the more toxic it is likely to be. The toxin also appears to accumulate in the human body as well, which means that a person could, after several meals of marginally toxic fish, build up to a noticeable or even dangerous case of ciguatera poisoning. Recovery usually takes nine days, but in May 1988 medical researchers announced the discovery of a potentially effective treatment or cure for ciguatera. A sugar compound called manitol—which is widely used in medicine as a diuretic—appears to produce dramatic recovery within minutes of its injection.

Symptoms usually occur within 30 minutes to twelve hours, and include abdominal pain and diarrhea; nausea and vomiting; a tingling or numbness in the nose, lips, tongue and throat; a metallic or peppery taste in the mouth; joint aches; headache and dizziness; cyanosis (skin turning blue); weakness; pain or sensation of looseness in the teeth; visual disturbances; difficulty urinating; itching and skin rash; blisters and sloughing of skin; convulsions; hypersensitivity to heat and cold or a reversal of hot/cold sensations; death (7 percent mortality rate).

Suspect fish include approximately four hundred species, but most cases of ciguatoxic poisoning have been traced to a relatively few species. In North America and Caribbean waters, the following species account for almost all cases of ciguatera poisoning, especially those listed in bold face:

Barracudas (Sphyraenidae), esp. **Great Barracuda (*Sphyraena barracuda*)**

Silk Snapper (*Lutjanus vivanus*)
Dog Snapper (*Lutjanus jocu*)
Certain other Snappers (esp. *Lutjanus spp.*)
Greater Amberjack (*Seriola dumerili*)
Other Jacks (esp. *Caranx spp.*)
King Mackerel (*Scomberomorus cavalla*)
Black Grouper (*Mycteroperca bonaci*)
Yellowfin Grouper (*Mycteroperca venenosa*)
Certain other Groupers (esp. *Epinephelus spp.*)
Morays (Muraenidae)
Hogfishes (Labridae)
Parrotfishes (Scaridae)
Wrasses (Labridae)
Surgeonfishes (Acanthuridae)

Hallucinogenic Fish Poisoning (Ichthyoallyeinotoxic Fish)

This poisoning is usually associated with tropical reef fish from the Indian and Pacific oceans, and the toxin is reported to be strongest in the head of the fish. Because fish bearing this toxin often also carry ciguatoxin, the two poisons may be related.

Symptoms develop within minutes or hours, and may last for several days: dizziness and loss of motor coordination; hallucinations; depression; chest constriction; itching or burning throat; weakness.

Suspect fish include:

Groupers (Serranidae)
Surgeonfishes (Acanthuridae)
Chubs (Kyphosidae)
Mullets (Mugilidae)
Goatfishes (Mullidae)
Sergeant Majors (Pomacentridae)
Rabbitfishes (Siganidae)

Clupeotoxic Poisoning

Most ichthyotoxins are associated with bottom-feeders or their predators, but this poison is found in the flesh of the mostly plankton-feeding members of the order Clupeiformes. It occurs within the same regions as ciguatera, but less frequently.

Symptoms are usually rapid and violent, and include nausea and vomiting; a dryness or metallic taste in the mouth; weak pulse; abdominal pain and diarrhea; emotional hypertension; headache; tingling sensations or numbness; coma; death (possibly within fifteen minutes; mortality rate is greater than 45 percent).

Suspect fish include:

Herrings (Clupeidae)
Sardines (Clupeidae)
Tarpon and relatives (Elopidae): e.g., Ladyfish, Machete, Oxeye Herring
Anchovies (Engraulidae)

Paralytic Shellfish Poisoning (Saxitoxin)

Because most saltwater fishermen are fond of shellfish, I have chosen to list this toxin that afflicts the digestive organs, dark meat, gills, and siphons of shellfish during the dinoflagellate blooms that are called red tides. Cooking, especially panfrying, can remove up to 70 percent of the toxin; but, since some poisoning will still occur, it is best to heed red-tide alerts.

Symptoms that generally appear within thirty minutes may include a tingling or burning sensation of the lips, gums, tongue, and face, perhaps spreading to the neck, arms, hands, and legs; numbness; loss of motor coordination, accompanied by a feeling of "lightness"; headache; dizziness; weakness; throat constriction; incoherent speech; diarrhea and abdominal pain; a sensation that one's teeth are loose or "set on edge"; temporary blindness; respiratory paralysis and death (10 to 35 percent mortality rate, usually within twelve hours).

Suspect species include:

Most Bivalves (Pelecypoda), e.g., Clams, Mussels, Oysters, Cockles, Scallops, etc.
Chitons (Mopalidae)
Limpets (Acmaediae)
Murexes (Muricidae)
Periwinkles (Littorinidae)
Sand Crabs (Hippidae)
Barnacles (Thoracica)

TOXINS PRODUCED BY SPOILAGE OR DECOMPOSITION

Virtually any fish or shellfish can cause "food poisoning" if the flesh is not handled carefully. Bacteria, molds, and yeasts are the usual agents of the toxicity, but bacterial food poisoning is thought to be by far the most common type of fish or seafood poisoning. To prevent bacterial food poisoning from fish, the catch should be gutted and cleaned immediately after it is caught, and either eaten or properly preserved as soon thereafter as possible. Next safest approach is to get the freshly caught fish on ice right away. Never store fish or seafood—whole, cleaned, or even cooked—at warm temperatures, above 40°F, say. And that also includes fish on a stringer or in a live well in typical fishing-temperature water. You can expect bacterial decompositon to begin as soon as the fish die.

Never eat fish or shellfish that looks suspicious, feels slimy, smells bad, or tastes funny, especially if it tastes peppery or sharp.

Certain spoilage toxins are common enough and serious enough to merit a brief discussion here.

Scombroid Poisoning

This bacterial poisoning occurs in improperly preserved mackerels, tunas, sardines, anchovies, wahoo, sauries, and perhaps other dark-meated marine fish such as bluefish. Too often, scombrotoxicity occurs after such fish have been left in the sun for two hours or so. The muscle tissue of these dark-meated fish contains a chemical known as histidine, which bacterial decomposition converts to histamine and saurine. These chemicals, and particularly the latter, cause an allergic reaction, the symptoms and severity of which vary considerably from person to person. Unlike other fish-spoilage toxins, these bacteria and chemicals may produce very little evidence of putrefaction other than a sharp peppery taste to the meat. Other possible signs include pallid gills and an "off" odor.

Ptomaine Poisoning

This term covers a rather wide range of bacterial poisons, but the ones to watch out for in fish and shellfish are three: botulism, staphylococcus, and streptococcus. Symptoms vary considerably, but usually include nausea and vomiting, diarrhea and abdominal pain, headache, chills, fever, muscular aches, weakness, sometimes shock. In botulism cases, add slurred speech, blurred vision, respiratory distress, muscular paralysis, and death. Immediate cleaning of the catch, low-temperature (35 to 40°) storage for the short term, careful preservation (freezing, canning, pickling, drying, smoking, and so forth) over longer periods, and recooking leftovers, especially those with dark meat, are the procedures for avoiding these toxins:

Botulism can occur in salted or smoke-dried fish as well as in fresh seafood. The symptoms of botulism occur in eight to seventy-two hours and, in something like 65 percent of cases, lead to death. Fortunately, there exists an antitoxin (if you can get it in time), and the anaerobic bacterium responsible for botulism can be killed by exposure to heat: 250°F (meat temperature, not oven temperature) for four to five minutes is usually all it takes.

Staphylococcus is the most common source of food poisoning, but isn't very often fatal. Symptoms of distress appear within one to six hours and usually last only one to three days, their severity being extremely variable. Some people even seem to be able to build up a resistance to this enterotoxin. The bacterium can withstand boiling temperatures for up to thirty minutes, and most cases stem from improper canning.

Streptococcus affects fish and shellfish stored at warm temperatures. Symptoms occur within two to eighteen hours and are fortunately rather mild, for no effective treatment is known.

POISONS CAUSED BY POLLUTION

These poisons are, unfortunately, becoming more and more common. Only vigilant enforcement of clean-water laws and other antipollution standards can stem and turn the tide.

Perhaps the oldest form of seafood poisoning by pollution is **hepatitis,** caused by eating the viscera of fish or shellfish that have been living in waters polluted by sewage, agricultural wastes, and storm or barnyard runoff containing coliform bacteria. Clams, oysters, and mussels are the species most often involved, but primarily because they are the most popular seafoods eaten whole, gut and all. Any filter-feeding organism that dwells in sewage-polluted water is a primary candidate for causing hepatitis, and even finfish that are eaten whole (whitebait, smelts, and the like) may not be safe if the water isn't. Cooking does not remove the danger.

In recent years, the list of pollutant poisons fouling our waters and the fish that swim in them has increased dramatically. Some of them are especially dangerous in fish and shellfish tissues that concentrate the chemicals: livers, kidneys, gonads, roe, milt, and other parts of the viscera, and the dark, often bloody or oily, meat concentrated here and there about a fish's body. Unfortunately, many of them render the muscular tissue or flesh itself unsafe to eat. The most common pollutants that affect fish and shellfish include pesticides, PCBs, fertilizers, heavy metals (mercury, copper, lead, and the like), solvents, petrochemicals, pharmaceuticals, radioactive materials, acids—you name it. The sources of these pollutants are legion: seepage from dumps and landfills; sewage outfalls (treated or not) and sewage-treatment-plant sludge; highways and railroads; refineries and factories; construction sites and rubble dumps; mine tailings and processing-plant dumps; settling ponds; runoff from farms, feedlots, even streets and lawns; storm sewers; industrial and municipal wastes of every sort.

Anglers ought to be (but all too seldom are) among the most active environmentalists. Fish can't complain or sue or vote, but fishermen can. Our license fees aren't enough that we can expect the state fishery agencies and commissions to do the work for us. And in most coastal states we saltwater anglers aren't contributing anything at all to management, protection, and mitigation, because we don't have to buy saltwater licenses.

KEEPING FISH FRESH, SAFE, AND EDIBLE

The prevention of fish spoilage and the preservation of a fish's freshness and palatability begin almost as soon as the shouting dies down. The best plan is to gut fish, remove their gills, and get them on ice as soon as they are caught. But few of us have the discipline to do that while we are fishing. So, the next-best plan is to ice them down whole, immediately. Third-best approach is to keep them alive. The worst plan by far is to let them die on a stringer, in a fish box, or on the bank.

Let me say it again: Water that is of a temperature for fishing is a perfect medium for bacterial growth. Don't keep dead fish on a stringer, in a fish well, or in the summer air—particularly if their guts and gills are still in place. Get them on ice!

If you use a creel, gut and de-gill your trout or other fish as soon as possible, keep them cool in moss, and don't count on their keeping that way more than two or three hours.

To keep fish deliciously and safely fresh, you should chill them as quickly as possible to just above freezing, 33°F. The best way to do that is to surround the fish completely in chipped or shaved ice. Ice cubes aren't good enough, and block ice is next to worthless. The amount of ice required depends upon the weight of the fish and the temperature of their flesh when the process begins. You can chill fifteen pounds of lake trout taken from 45°F water with as little as one or two pounds of shaved ice. If the fish are taken from 65°F water, it will take three to four pounds of ice—that is assuming the ice and the fish are in a covered, and preferably insulated, box. If the box is uncovered, you will need at least twice as much ice. Have ice touching the fish everywhere. Add the ice and the fish in alternate layers. And keep the meltwater draining.

Having gotten your fish down close to freezing—and it won't take that long, if you are using enough ice—block ice in a foam or similar container will suffice to keep it at that temperature. Again, the ice requirement varies, this time with the weight of the fish and the air temperature. That nice, fifteen-pound catch of lake trout will require a two-pound block of ice if the day is a chilly 50°F. Add a pound for every ten degrees (for example, six pounds at 90°F). If your fish box is not insulated, it will take two to three times as much ice.

To **freeze** fish properly, carefully wrap each serving-size portion individually, being sure that each package is airtight. (Really fastidious types dip them first in a superchilling briny slush. And some trout fishermen I know freeze each trout separately in a quart milk carton full of water.) I like to wrap them first in plastic wrap, then in freezer paper. Mark the date and species on each package. Under the best conditions, oily species will retain their fresh taste for a maximum of three months; very lean species can be kept for about a year. The proper freezer temperature is 0°F or colder. Virtually no refrigerator freezer compartment can maintain that low a temperature, so don't plan to keep frozen fish there longer than two to four weeks. Foods freeze fastest when the unfrozen packages are not touching one another. Once they are frozen, proximity is no problem.

When you **thaw** frozen fish, do it in the refrigerator. And let any meltwater drain off the thawing fish. If your thin fillets are individually wrapped, you can thaw them fast at room temperature. But that is not a safe procedure for whole, pan-dressed fish, big steaks, or thick fillets.

Treat fish with the respect they deserve, and you will have no trouble with "food-poisoning" caused by spoilage. And long before bacteria and chemical decomposition make fish toxic, they certainly render it unpalatable. Most people who say they don't like fish feel that way only because they've never had truly fresh fish.

A SUMMARY OF IGFA RULES AND REGULATIONS

Most anglers think of the International Game Fishing Association as merely the arbiter of world-record applications and keeper of the records, but the IGFA is a great deal more than that. What began as a rather elite organization for high-minded and well-heeled seekers of big-game fishing records has become the preeminent sportfishing organization in the world. Yes, IGFA still accepts or rejects world-record applications, and still keeps and publishes those records, but it also sets the rules for ethical sportfishing in fresh and salt water, even fly-fishing. Unless a person is applying for a world record, these rules aren't legally or technically enforceable—each state sets its own seasons, limits and other fishing regulations, and on the high seas almost anything goes—but the sporting angler would do well to follow them. In only one respect—the ban against using wire lines for trolling—are IGFA's rules more stringent than necessary.

(That ban has always been a subject of some heated controversy, particularly among saltwater anglers from the northeastern corner of the United States.)

IGFA's rules committee reviews the rules, regulations, and record requirements each year, and sometimes makes changes. The summary that follows pertains to those rules that cover the 1988 angling season. They are divided into four sections: General Rules; Special Rules for Fly-Fishing; Disqualifying Acts or Situations; World-Record Requirements. For more detailed information about these rules or about membership in IGFA, write to International Game Fishing Association, 3000 E. Las Olas Blvd., Fort Lauderdale, FL 33316.

GENERAL RULES FOR FISHING IN FRESH AND SALT WATER

Equipment Regulations:

In general, IGFA's equipment rules are designed to not give the angler any unfair advantage in hooking, fighting, or landing a fish. Such unfair advantages include the use of mechanically aided tackle or gear that increases the likelihood of foul-hooking fish.

Line: Monofilament, multifilament, and lead-core lines may be used; wire lines are prohibited. See *World Record Requirements* for line classes.

Line Backing: If backing is attached to the line, it may not exceed the 60 kg. (130 lb.) class and must be of one of the approved line types above; a catch will be classified under the heavier of the two lines. If the backing is *not* attached to the line, anything goes.

Double Line: If one is used, it must consist of the actual line used to catch the fish and meet certain dimensional criteria, measured inclusive of the knots, splices, or hardware at either end.

Leader: If a leader is used it may be made of any material in any strength but its overall length, inclusive of any lure, hook, rig, or other piece of terminal tackle, must also meet certain dimensional criteria. If **both** double line and leader are used, you can't just add the allowable maximum lengths for each, because the maximum combined length allowed is shorter. Let these drawings tell the story:

Freshwater Species—All Classes of Tackle

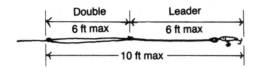

Saltwater Species—All Classes Up To and Including 20 lb. (10 kg.)

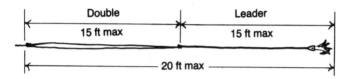

Saltwater Species—All Classes Over 20 lb. (10 kg.)

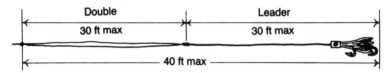

Rod: Considerable latitude is allowed, but the rod must comply with sporting ethics and customs and may not give the angler an unfair advantage. This rule is intended to eliminate the use of "trick" rods. The following required rod dimensions are made in both directions from a point directly beneath the center of the reel. Curved butts are measured in a straight line.

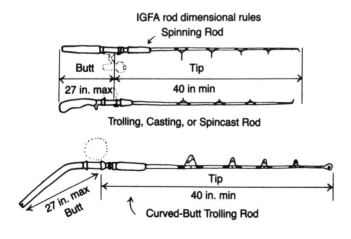

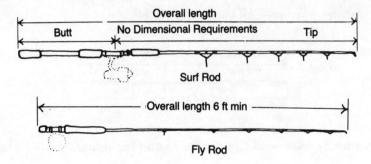

Surf Rod

Fly Rod

Reel: Reels, too, must comply with sporting ethics and customs. That means no ratchet handles, no double handles that can be cranked with both hands at the same time, no power-driven reels, nothing that would give the angler an unfair advantage.

Hooks for Bait Fishing: Single hooks only; no double- or treble-barbed hooks may be used when fishing live or dead bait. *Tandem hook arrangements and two-hook bottom-fishing rigs* are okay, subject to certain requirements as to their distance apart (however, the point of one hook may pass through the eye of the other). Hooks must be firmly imbedded in or securely attached to the bait; swinging or dangling hooks are prohibited.

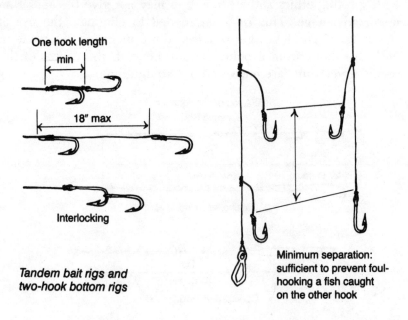

Tandem bait rigs and two-hook bottom rigs

Minimum separation: sufficient to prevent foul-hooking a fish caught on the other hook

Hooks and Lures: On artificial lures that have skirts or trailing material, no more than two single hooks may be attached to the line or leader. Unless the point of one hook is passed through the eye of the other, the two hooks are subject to certain separation requirements. The trailing hook may not extend more than a hook's length beyond the skirt of the lure.

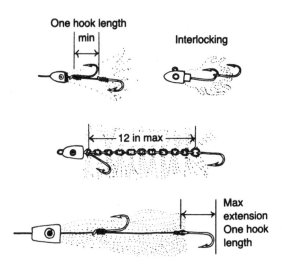

Hooks and lures

In the case of plugs or other lures expressly designed for their use, gang hooks may be used so long as they are free-swinging and number no more than three (single, double, or treble hooks, or a combination of the three).

Other Equipment: *Fighting chairs, rod belts, waist gimbals, fighting harnesses, and safety lines* are okay, so long as the gimbals are free-swinging, harnesses are not attached to fighting chairs, and nothing is mechanically aided or otherwise designed to provide unusual advantage or let the angler rest during the fight. Unless the angler is fishing from a bridge, pier, or other high platform, *gaffs or nets* used to boat or land a fish may not exceed eight feet (2.43 meters) in length, and on *flying or detachable gaffs,* the rope must not exceed thirty feet (9.14 meters). *Snags and other entangling devices,* with or without a hook, may not be used in baiting, hooking, fighting, or landing a fish. *Outriggers, downriggers, and kites* are permitted, so long as the actual fishing line, **not** the leader or double line, is attached to the snap or other release device. A small *float* may be used to regulate the depth of the bait, but any flotation device that in any way hampers the fighting ability of the fish is prohibited.

Angling Regulations:

IGFA's rules on angling are designed to make the angler do most of the work, with only very limited help from the boat, the fish, or anyone else. From the time the fish strikes or takes a bait, the angler **alone** must hook and fight the fish, and the assistance allowed in landing or boating the fish is limited and carefully defined.

   Striking: The angler is supposed to strike and hook the fish with the rod in hand, so the angler must remove the rod from any *rod holder* in use as quickly as possible after a fish strikes. In the event of a *multiple strike* on separate lines, only the first fish fought by any angler will be considered for a world record.

   Fighting: The fish should be fought on the single line most of the time it takes to land the fish, not on the double line or heavy leader.

   Assistance: The *harness*, if used, may be replaced or adjusted by a person other than the angler. *When angling from a boat,* once the leader is brought within the grasp of the mate or is wound to the rod tip, more than one person is permitted to hold the leader. *One or more gaffers* may be used in addition to the person(s) holding the leader.

SPECIAL RULES FOR FLY-FISHING

Equipment Regulations:

Generally accepted fly-fishing customs prevail here, to help preserve the distinction between fly-fishing and other forms of angling.

   Line: Any type of fly line and backing may be used.

   Leader: Leaders must conform to generally accepted fly-fishing customs. A Leader includes a *class tippet*, an optional *shock tippet*, and a *butt or taper section* between the fly line and the class tippet. There are no limits on the strength, length, or material of the butt or taper section, but the other parts of the leader must conform to certain limits.

   Class Tippet: The class tippet must be made of nonmetallic ma-

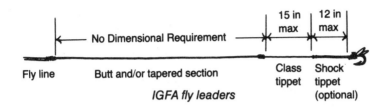

terial and attached directly to either the fly or, if one is used, the shock tippet. Its *length* must be at least fifteen inches (38.1 cm.), measured inside the connecting knots; no maximum length. The breaking strength determines the class of the tippet. (In the case of knotless tapered leaders used without separate class tippets, the terminal fifteen inches [38.1 cm.] will determine tippet class.)

Shock Tippet: A shock tippet, made of any material and without any limit on its breaking strength, may be attached to the class tippet and tied to the fly. *Length* may not exceed twelve inches (30.48 cm.), measured from the eye of the hook to the single strand of class tippet, including any knots used.

Rod: Regardless of the material used or the number of sections, the rod must conform to generally accepted fly-fishing customs and practices, and must not give the angler any unsporting advantage. *Minimum overall length* is six feet (1.82 meters).

Reel: The reel must be designed expressly for fly-fishing and cannot be used in casting the fly other than as a storage spool for the line. Gear ratios and drag types are not restricted except where the angler would gain an unfair advantage. Electric or electronically operated reels are prohibited.

Hooks: A conventional fly may be dressed on a single or double hook, or two single hooks in tandem. Treble hooks are prohibited. The second hook in a *tandem-hook fly* must not extend beyond

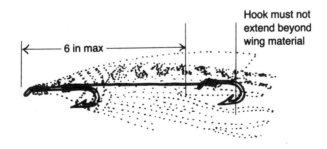

Tandem-hook fly

the wing material, and the eyes of the hooks may be no farther apart than six inches (15.24 cm.).

Lures: The lure must be a recognized type of artificial fly—dry fly, wet fly, nymph, streamer, bucktail, bug, popper, tube fly. No miniature plugs, plastic worms or minnows, or other dubious, fly-rod-sized artificials are permitted. Nor may natural or preserved baits be used, alone or to tip a fly.

Gaffs and Nets: Only fixed, single-hook gaffs may be used; flying gaffs are prohibited. Otherwise, the same regulations prevail as outlined above.

Angling Regulations:

The angler must cast the fly, and hook, fight, and bring the fish to gaff or net unaided by any other person. No one else may touch any part of the tackle during the playing of the fish or give aid other than taking the leader for gaffing or netting.

Casting and retrieving: Must conform to normal customs and generally accepted practices. The major criterion in casting is that the weight of the line must carry the lure rather than the weight of the lure carrying the line. *Trolling* a lure behind a moving water craft is not permitted. The boat or craft must be completely out of gear both at the time the fly is presented to the fish and during the retrieve.

Fighting: Once a fish is hooked, the tackle may not be altered in any way, except to add an *extension butt*. Fish must be hooked on *the lure in use;* if a small fish takes the lure and a larger fish swallows the smaller one, the catch will be disqualified.

Assistance: One or more people may assist in *gaffing or netting the fish*.

DISQUALIFYING ACTS OR SITUATIONS

The following acts or situations will disqualify a catch:

1. Failure to comply with the equipment or angling regulations specified above.

2. The act of persons other than the angler touching any part of the rod, reel, or line (including any double line), either bodily or with any device, during the playing of the fish, or in giving aid other than that allowed in the rules and regulations. (If any obsta-

cle to the passage of the line through the rod guides has to be removed from the line, then the obstacle—whether chum, float-line, rubber band, weed, flotsam, or other material—shall be held and cut free; under no circumstances should the line be held or touched by anyone other than the angler during this process.)

3. Resting the rod in a rod holder, on the gunwale or any other part of the boat, or in or on any other object while playing the fish.

4. Hand-lining or using a hand line or rope attached in any manner to the angler's line or leader for the purpose of holding or lifting the fish.

5. Intentionally foul-hooking or snagging a fish.

6. Shooting, harpooning, or lancing the fish being played (including sharks) prior to landing or boating the fish.

7. Chumming with the flesh, blood, skin, or any part of mammals; additionally, using as bait the flesh, blood, skin, or any part of mammals other than hair or pork rind, or using a size or kind of bait that is illegal to possess.

8. Using a boat or device to beach or drive a fish into shallow water in order to deprive the fish of its normal ability to swim.

9. Attaching the angler's line or leader to part of a boat or other object for the purpose of holding or lifting the fish.

10. Changing the rod or reel while the fish is being played.

11. Splicing, removing, or adding to the line while the fish is being played.

12. Catching a fish in a manner that the double line never leaves the rod tip.

13. If a fish escapes before gaffing or netting and is recaptured by any method other than as outlined in the angling rules.

14. If a rod breaks (while the fish is being played) in a manner that reduces its length (or the length of the tip) below minimum dimensions or severely impairs its angling characteristics.

15. When a fish is hooked on more than one line.

16. Mutilation to the fish, prior to its landing or boating, caused by sharks, other fish, mammals, or propellors that remove or penetrate the flesh. (Injuries caused by leader or line, scratches, old healed scars, or regeneration deformities are not considered disqualifying injuries.) Any mutilation on the fish must be shown in a photograph and fully explained in a separate report accompanying a record application.

WORLD RECORD REQUIREMENTS

Any fish considered for world-record status must have been caught according to the International Angling Rules outlined above. IGFA maintains world records for both freshwater and saltwater game fishes in line class, tippet class, and all-tackle categories. In line-class and tippet-class categories, only certain species are elegible, roughly seventy-five species each from fresh water and salt water (too many to list here), and new species are added from time to time. For each of these species, a maximum line class is specified. (Prior to the institution of this rule, the record book was polluted with too many records of light fish having been taken on heavy tackle.) The requirements and regulations concerning world record catches are so detailed they don't lend themselves to easy summary. Anglers hoping to be enshrined in the record book had better write to IGFA for a copy of the rules. Better still, join up, so you can get the bimonthly newsletter and keep up with all the changes as they occur. Here are the general requirements for world records.

Weights: To qualify for a record, a fish must weigh at least one pound (0.453 kg.) or meet the minimum acceptance weights that have been established for many vacant record categories, and outweigh an existing record by the specified amount (two ounces for fish weighing less than twenty-five pounds, or one half of one percent of the existing record for fish weighing twenty-five pounds or more). If a fish matches or tops an existing record by less than the required weight, it will be listed as a tie. Estimated weights are not accepted, and fractions of ounces (or their metric equivalents) are not considered in breaking ties.

Conditions of the Catch: Fish may not be caught in hatchery waters or sanctuaries, and the catch must conform to any laws or regulations governing the species or the waters in which it was caught.

All-Tackle Category: Such world records are kept for the heaviest fish of a species caught by an angler in any class up to 130 pounds (60 kg.), including species not eligible for line-class or tippet-class records (subject to certain restrictions).

Line-Class Categories: Line-class records are maintained for more than 150 species according to the **wet** testing strength of the line used by the angler. With the exception of all-tackle record claims, line classes are limited to certain maximum classes for many species. Records are kept in the following line-class categories:

1 kg.	2 lb.
2 kg.	4 lb.
4 kg.	8 lb.
6 kg.	12 lb.
8 kg.	16 lb.
10 kg.	20 lb.
15 kg.	30 lb.
24 kg.	50 lb.
37 kg.	80 lb.
60 kg.	130 lb.

Fly-Rod or Tippet-Class Categories: Fly-rod world records are maintained according to tipped strength. Records are kept for the same species as for line-class records, but in the following tippet classes:

1 kg.	2 lb.
2 kg.	4 lb.
4 kg.	8 lb.
6 kg.	12 lb.
8 kg.	16 lb.

Line and Tippet Testing: Line, leader, and tippet samples must accompany all world-record claims, and IGFA tests them all. Such tests are conducted according to government specifications that have been modified and supplemented by IGFA. The maximum strengths allowed for each class are as follows:

1.00 kg.	2.20 lb.
2.00 kg.	4.40 lb.
4.00 kg.	8.81 lb.
6.00 kg.	13.22 lb.
8.00 kg.	17.63 lb.
10.00 kg.	22.04 lb.
15.00 kg.	33.06 lb.
24.00 kg.	52.91 lb.
37.00 kg.	81.57 lb.
60.00 kg.	132.27 lb.

Regulations Governing Record Catches:

Like most certifying organizations, IGFA reserves the right to investigate claims, adjudicate protests and disputes, and make final decisions.

Species Identification: Hybrids and species that may pose a problem of identity should be examined by an ichthyologist or qualified fishery biologist before a record or contest application is submitted, and his signature should appear on the application form or separate document. If there is the slightest doubt that the species can be positively identified from the photograph and other data submitted, the fish should be retained in a preserved or frozen condition. In cases of doubtful species identity, and with no proof having been submitted by the angler, photographs of the catch will be submitted to qualified ichthyologists for decisions; if the species cannot be positively identified, the record claim will not be considered.

Witnesses: If at all possible, witnesses to the claimed record catch are highly desirable, especially if they can attest to the angler's compliance with IGFA angling and equipment regulations.

Time Limits: With the exception of all-tackle records, claims for record fish must be received by IGFA within certain time limits, depending upon where the fish were caught: *In continental United States waters,* within sixty days of the date of the catch. *In other waters,* within three months of the date of the catch. The rules allow for *incomplete record claims* to be submitted within the specified time limits, so long as the reasons are due to circumstances beyond the angler's control and are fully explained, and the missing data are supplied within a reasonable time. *All-tackle records only* are considered for catches made in past years if (1) acceptable photographs are submitted, (2) the weight of the fish can be positively verified, (3) the method of catch can be substantiated, and (4) the information and substantiating data supplied are deemed adequate.

Weighing Requirements: IGFA's weighing requirements are fairly complicated, to take into account the varying conditions that exist throughout the world. Here in the United States, the smart record seeker would have his fish weighed by an official weighmaster or IGFA official, in the presence of disinterested witnesses, on scales that have been checked and certified for accuracy within the last twelve months by a government agency or duly accredited organization. No matter where or how the fish is weighed, only weights indicated by the graduations on the scales are accepted. Any weights that fall between these graduations must be rounded downward. Fish weighed only at sea or on other bodies of water will not be accepted as records. At the time of the weighing, the actual *tackle used* by the angler to catch the fish must be exhibited to weighmaster and witnesses. And, incidentally, all angling and equipment regulations apply until the fish is actually weighed; no claiming that a fish was mutilated by the marina's derrick or the weighmaster's winch.

Application Procedures: A record claim must be submitted on an official IGFA world-record application form or a full-size reproduction, which must be filled in by the angler personally. The angler is responsible for securing the necessary signatures and addresses of boat captain, weighmaster, and witnesses. The specified strength of the line or tippet used to catch the fish **must** be specified on the form. The angler must appear in person to have the application notarized. The application must be accompanied by the required line, leader, and tippet samples, photographs or sketches of the lure or multiple-hook bait rig used to catch the fish (in the case of fly-fishing records, the actual fly that caught the fish must still be attached to the tippet sample), and photographs of the fish (both hanging and lying on its side), the tackle used to catch the fish, the actual scales used to weigh the fish, and the angler with the fish. The requirements for each of these enclosures are fairly specific. *Deliberate falsification* of an application will result in disqualification of the applicant for any future IGFA world record and nullification of any existing records.

That's the gist of it, but if you have any reason to believe you have a potential record catch, better get in touch with IGFA in a hurry.

CONVERSION TABLES, FACTORS, AND FORMULAS

Now that nearly everyone else in the world is on the metric system, and we've sort of wetted our toes a bit in metrics, things can get confusing—especially if you go to buy tackle that was manufactured abroad. Some fishing tackle is labeled in metric units, some in U.S. customary units, and some in both systems. Until we get our metric act together, anglers will need to make conversions from time to time. This section is devoted to the various factors and formulas you need to switch back and forth between the metric and customary systems.

Besides the obvious problem of units, there are other problems in switching back and forth between the two measurement systems. In America, we tend to use fractions to express measurements that fall between our whole units, whereas metric users prefer decimals. So, let us begin there, with converting fractions to their decimal equivalents.

FRACTIONS AND THEIR DECIMAL EQUIVALENTS

1/64	0.016	17/64	0.266	33/64	0.516	49/64	0.766
1/32	.031	9/32	.281	17/32	.531	25/32	.781
3/64	.047	19/64	.297	35/64	.547	51/64	.797
1/16	.063	3/10	.300	9/16	.563	4/5	.800
5/64	.078	5/16	.313	37/64	.578	13/16	.813
3/32	.094	21/64	.328	19/32	.594	53/64	.828
1/10	.100	1/3	.333	3/5	.600	5/6	.833
7/64	.109	11/32	.344	39/64	.609	27/32	.844
1/8	.125	23/64	.359	5/8	.625	55/64	.859
9/64	.141	3/8	.375	41/64	.641	7/8	.875
5/32	.156	25/64	.391	21/32	.656	57/64	.891
1/6	.167	2/5	.400	2/3	.667	9/10	.900
11/64	.172	13/32	.406	43/64	.672	29/32	.906
3/16	.188	27/64	.422	11/16	.688	59/64	.922
1/5	.200	7/16	.438	7/10	.700	15/16	.938
13/64	.203	29/64	.453	45/64	.703	61/64	.953
7/32	.219	15/32	.469	23/32	.719	31/32	.967
15/64	.234	31/64	.484	47/64	.734	63/64	.984
1/4	.250	1/2	.500	3/4	.750		

INCHES EXPRESSED AS DECIMAL PARTS OF FEET

Ordinarily, we express parts of feet as inches, and parts of inches in fractions. It is very difficult to use these units and fractions in mathematical computations. When they are expressed as decimal parts of feet, such calculations are much easier.

Inches	Feet	Inches		Inches	Feet
1/16	0.005	0.062		3	0.250
1/8	.010	.125		4	.333
1/4	.021	.250		5	.417
3/8	.031	.375		6	.500
1/2	.042	.500		7	.583
5/8	.052	.625		8	.667
3/4	.063	.750		9	.750
7/8	.073	.875		10	.833
1	.083	1.000		11	.917
2	.167			12	1.000

TEMPERATURE CONVERSION BETWEEN CELSIUS AND FAHRENHEIT

Increasingly, and especially in writings of a scientific nature, the metric Celsius scale is being used rather than our Fahrenheit scale for temperatures. Converting from one scale to the other is not particularly difficult.

Fahrenheit to Celsius:
Multiply the Celsius temperature by 1.8 and add 32

$$°C \times 1.8 + 32 = °F$$

Celsius to Fahrenheit:
Subtract 32 from the Fahrenheit temperature, then multiply the result by 0.556

$$(°F - 32) \times 0.556 = °C$$

Here are a few good temperatures to remember:

Freezing Point of Water:	0° C, 32° F
Boiling Point of Water:	100° C, 212° F

Human Body Temperature:	37° C, 98.6° F
Winter Lake Temperature:	4° C, 39° F
Very Hot Summer Day:	32° C, 90° F
Very Cold Winter Day:	−18° C, 0° F

The temperature conversion table on pages 152–153 is even easier to use.

USEFUL CONVERSION FACTORS

Weight

1 kilogram (kg) = 1000 grams (gm) = 2.2 pounds (lb) = 35.3 ounces (oz)

1 gram (gm) = 0.001 kilogram (kg) = 1000 milligrams (mg) = 15.432 grains (gr) = 0.035 ounce (oz)

1 milligram (mg) = 0.015 grains (gr)

1 grain (gr) = 64.799 milligrams (mg)

1 microgram (μg) = 0.000001 gram (gm)

1 pound (lb) = 16 ounces (oz) = 0.454 kilogram (kg)

1 ounce (oz) = 0.063 pound (lb) = 437.5 grains (gr) = 28.35 grams (gm) = 0.028 kilogram (kg)

Length, Distance

1 micron (μ) = 0.001 millimeter (mm) = 0.00003937 inch (in)

1 millimeter (mm) = 0.1 centimeter (cm) = 0.001 meter (m) = 0.039 inch (in)

1 centimeter (cm) = 10 millimeters (mm) = 0.01 meter (m) = 0.394 inch (in)

1 meter (m) = 1000 millimeters (mm) = 100 centimeters (cm) = 39.37 inches (in) = 3.28 feet (ft) = 1.09 yards (yd)

1 kilometer (km) = 1000 meters (m) = 0.621 statute land miles (mi) = 0.54 nautical miles (nm)

1 mil = 0.001 inch (in) = 0.0254 millimeter (mm)

1 inch (in) = 0.083 foot (ft) = 25.4 millimeters (mm) = 2.54 centimeters (cm)

1 foot (ft) = 12 inches (in) = 0.333 yard (yd) = 30.48 centimeters (cm) = 0.305 meter (m)

1 yard (yd) = 36 inches (in) = 3 feet (ft) = 91.44 centimeters (cm) = 0.914 meter (m)

1 fathom (f) = 6 feet (ft) = 182.88 centimeters (cm) = 1.829 meters (m)

1 statute mile (mi) = 5280 feet (ft) = 1760 yards (yd) = 0.869 nautical miles (nm) = 1609 meters (m) = 1.609 kilometers (km)

1 nautical mile (nm) = 6076.115 feet (ft) = 1.151 statute miles (mi) = 1852 meters (m) = 1.852 kilometers (km)

Speed

1 centimeter per second (cps or cm/sec) = 0.01 meter per second (mps or m/sec) = 0.394 inches per second (ips) = 0.033 feet per second (fps)

1 meter per second (mps or m/sec) = 100 centimeters per second (cps or cm/sec) = 3.6 kilometers per hour (kph) = 3.28 feet per second (fps) = 2.24 miles per hour (mph) = 1.94 knots (kt)

1 kilometer per hour (kph) = 0.278 meters per second (mps or m/sec) = 0.911 feet per second (fps) = 0.621 miles per hour (mph) = 0.54 knots (kt)

1 inch per second (ips) = 0.083 feet per second (fps) = 2.54 centimeters per second (cps or cm/sec)

1 foot per second (fps) = 0.682 miles per hour (mph) = 0.592 knots (kt) = 30.48 centimeters per second (cps or cm/sec) = 0.305 meters per second (mps or m/sec) = 1.1 kilometers per hour (kph)

1 mile per hour (mph) = 1.467 feet per second (fps) = 0.869 knots (kt) = 0.447 meters per second (mps or m/sec) = 1.609 kilometers per hour (kph)

1 knot (kt) = 1 nautical mile per hour (nm/hr) = 1.151 miles per hour (mph) = 1.688 feet per second (fps) = 1.852 kilometers per hour (kph) = 51.44 centimeters per second (cps or cm/sec) = 0.514 meters per second (mps or m/sec)

Area

1 square millimeter (mm^2) = 0.002 square inches (sq in or in^2)

1 square centimeter (cm^2) = 100 square millimeters (mm^2) = 0.155 square inches (sq in or in^2)

1 square meter (m^2) = 1,000,000 square millimeters (mm^2) = 10,000 square centimeters (cm^2) = 1550.003 square inches (sq in or in^2) = 10.764 square feet (sq ft or ft^2) = 1.196 square yards (sq yd or yd^2)

1 are (a) = 100 square meters (m^2) = 0.025 acre

1 hectare (ha) = 10,000 square meters (m^2) = 2.471 acres

1 square kilometer (km^2) = 100 hectares (ha) = 247.105 acres = 0.386 square mile (sq mi or mi^2)

1 square inch (sq in or in^2) = 6.452 square centimeters (cm^2)

1 square foot (sq ft or ft^2) = 144 square inches (sq in or in^2) = 929.03 square centimeters (cm^2) = 0.093 square meters (m^2)

1 square yard (sq yd or yd^2) = 9 square feet (sq ft or ft^2) = 1.2 square meters (m^2)

1 acre = 43,560 square feet (sq ft or ft^2) = 4046.856 square meters (m^2) = 0.405 hectares (ha)

1 square mile (sq mi or mi^2) = 1 section = 640 acres = 259 hectares (ha)

Volume

1 cubic centimeter (cc or cm^3) = 1 milliliter (ml) = 0.061 cubic inches (cu in or in^3) = 0.034 fluid ounces (fl oz)

1 liter (l) = 1000 cubic centimeters (cc or cm^3) = 0.001 cubic meter (m^3) = 61.024 cubic inches (cu in or in^3) = 33.814 fluid ounces (fl oz) = 1.057 liquid quarts (qt) = 0.264 liquid gallons (gal)

1 cubic meter (m^3) = 1000 liters (l) = 1,000,000 cubic centimeters (cc or cm^3) = 61,023.74 cubic inches (cu in or in^3) = 35.315 cubic feet (cu ft or ft^3) = 1.308 cubic yards (cu yd or yd^3) = 264.172 gallons (gal)

1 cubic inch (cu in or in^3) = 16.393 cubic centimeters (cc or cm^3)

1 cubic foot (cu ft or ft^3) = 1728 cubic inches (cu in or in^3) = 28,316.7 cubic centimeters (cc or cm^3) = 7.481 gallons (gal)

1 cubic yard (cu yd or yd^3) = 27 cubic feet (cu ft or ft^3) = 0.765 cubic meter (m^3)

1 fluid ounce (fl oz) = 1.805 cubic inches (cu in or in^3) = 29.573 cubic centimeters (cc or cm^3)

1 liquid quart (qt) = 32 fluid ounces (fl oz) = 0.946 liter (l)

1 dry quart (qt) = 1.101 liters (l)

1 gallon (gal) = 128 fluid ounces (fl oz) = 4 liquid quarts (qt) = 231 cubic inches (cu in or in^3) = 3.785 liters (l)

Pressure, Tensile Strength, etc.

1 pound per square inch (psi) = 0.7 grams per square millimeter (gm/mm^2) = 0.07 kilograms per square centimeter (kg/cm^2)

1000 pounds per square inch (1 kpsi or 1 ksi) = 0.7 kilograms per square centimeter (kg/cm^2)

CONVERSION FACTORS USED BY IGFA

Although the IGFA does not require that record applicants make any conversions (world record claims may be submitted in whatever weight and measurement units were taken at the time of the catch), *The IGFA Rule Book* lists these conversion formulas for weights and measures. Good usage dictates that numbers be rounded off to the same number of decimal points, but when it comes to dealing with fishing figures, it may be best to follow the IGFA's lead.

Ounces	x	28.349	= Grams
Ounces	x	0.02835	= Kilograms
Pounds	x	453.59	= Grams
Pounds	x	0.45359	= Kilograms
Grams	x	0.0353	= Ounces
Grams	x	0.002	= Pounds
Kilograms	x	35.2736	= Ounces
Kilograms	x	2.2046	= Pounds

Measures

Inches	x	25.4	= Millimeters
Inches	x	2.54	= Centimeters
Feet	x	30.48	= Centimeters
Feet	x	0.3048	= Meters
Millimeters	x	0.03937	= Inches
Centimeters	x	0.3937	= Inches
Centimeters	x	0.0328	= Feet
Meters	x	39.37	= Inches
Meters	x	3.28	= Feet
Fathoms	x	6	= Feet

Force

Pounds Force	x	4.448	= Newtons
Kilograms Force	x	9.806	= Newtons

CONVERSION TABLES

Useful as the above factors are in calculating conversion, it's faster using a table. Those that follow are designed for fast use and one-decimal-place accuracy, all that is practically needed in most angling situations.

To use these tables, find the figure that is known in the center column, then look in the appropriate column to left or right for the desired figure.

For example, in the first table, the Temperature Conversion Table, let us say that you have a temperature of 22 degrees Celsius and want to know the Fahrenheit temperature. Just find 22 in the center column, and look up the Fahrenheit temperature, 71.6 degrees, in the righthand column. If you know the Fahrenheit temperature, and want to calculate the Celsius, just find the known temperature and look in the lefthand column for the Celsius; if the known Fahrenheit temperature were still 22 degrees, the Celsius equivalent would be −5.6 degrees.

TEMPERATURE CONVERSION TABLE: CELSIUS/FAHRENHEIT

°C	Known	°F	°C	Known	°F	°C	Known	°F
−31.7	−25	−13.0	−8.3	17	62.6	3.9	39	102.2
−28.9	−20	−4.0	−7.8	18	64.4	4.4	40	104.0
−26.1	−15	5.0	−7.2	19	66.2	5.0	41	105.8
−23.4	−10	14.0	−6.7	20	68.0	5.6	42	107.6
−20.6	−5	23.0	−6.1	21	69.8	6.1	43	109.4
−17.8	0	32.0	−5.6	22	71.6	6.7	44	111.2
−17.2	1	33.8	−5.0	23	73.4	7.2	45	113.0
−16.7	2	35.6	−4.4	24	75.2	7.8	46	114.8
−16.1	3	37.4	−3.9	25	77.0	8.3	47	116.6
−15.6	4	39.2	−3.3	26	78.8	8.9	48	118.4
−15.0	5	41.0	−2.8	27	80.6	9.5	49	120.2
−14.5	6	42.8	−2.2	28	82.4	10.0	50	122.0
−13.9	7	44.6	−1.7	29	84.2	10.6	51	123.8
−13.3	8	46.4	−1.1	30	86.0	11.1	52	125.6
−12.8	9	48.2	−0.6	31	87.8	11.7	53	127.4
−12.2	10	50.0	0	32	89.6	12.2	54	129.2
−11.7	11	51.8	0.6	33	91.4	12.8	55	131.0
−11.1	12	53.6	1.1	34	93.2	13.3	56	132.8
−10.6	13	55.4	1.7	35	95.0	13.9	57	134.6
−10.0	14	57.2	2.2	36	96.8	14.5	58	136.4
−9.5	15	59.0	2.8	37	98.6	15.0	59	138.2
−8.9	16	60.8	3.3	38	100.4	15.6	60	140.0

°C	Known	°F	°C	Known	°F	°C	Known	°F
16.1	61	141.8	25.0	77	170.6	33.9	93	199.4
16.7	62	143.6	25.6	78	172.4	34.5	94	201.2
17.2	63	145.4	26.1	79	174.2	35.0	95	203.0
17.8	64	147.2	26.7	80	176.0	35.6	96	204.8
18.3	65	149.0	27.2	81	177.8	36.1	97	206.6
18.9	66	150.8	27.8	82	179.6	36.7	98	208.4
19.5	67	152.6	28.4	83	181.4	37.3	99	210.2
20.0	68	154.4	28.9	84	183.2	37.8	100	212.0
20.6	69	156.2	29.5	85	185.0	38.4	101	213.8
21.1	70	158.0	30.0	86	186.8	38.9	102	215.6
21.7	71	159.8	30.6	87	188.6	39.5	103	217.4
22.2	72	161.6	31.1	88	190.4	40.0	104	219.2
22.8	73	163.4	31.7	89	192.2	40.6	105	221.0
23.4	74	165.2	32.2	90	194.0	43.4	110	230.0
23.9	75	167.0	32.8	91	195.8	46.1	115	239.0
24.5	76	168.8	33.4	92	197.6	48.9	120	248.0

WEIGHT CONVERSION TABLE: POUNDS/KILOGRAMS

$$Lb \times 0.45359237 = Kg \qquad Kg \times 2.204623 = Lb$$

Lb	Known	Kg	Lb	Known	Kg	Lb	Known	Kg
2.2	1	0.5	59.5	27	12.2	143.3	65	29.5
4.4	2	0.9	61.7	28	12.7	154.3	70	31.8
6.6	3	1.4	63.9	29	13.2	165.3	75	34.0
8.8	4	1.8	66.1	30	13.6	176.4	80	36.3
11.0	5	2.3	68.3	31	14.1	187.4	85	38.6
13.2	6	2.7	70.5	32	14.5	198.4	90	40.8
15.4	7	3.2	72.8	33	15.0	209.4	95	43.1
17.6	8	3.6	75.0	34	15.4	220.5	100	45.4
19.8	9	4.1	77.2	35	15.9	242.5	110	49.9
22.0	10	4.6	79.4	36	16.3	275.6	125	56.7
24.3	11	5.0	81.6	37	16.8	330.7	150	68.0
26.5	12	5.4	83.8	38	17.2	385.8	175	79.4
28.7	13	5.9	86.0	39	17.7	440.9	200	90.7
30.9	14	6.4	88.2	40	18.1	496.0	225	102.1
33.1	15	6.8	90.4	41	18.6	551.2	250	113.4
35.3	16	7.3	92.6	42	19.1	606.3	275	124.7
37.5	17	7.7	94.8	43	19.5	661.4	300	136.1
39.7	18	8.2	97.0	44	20.0	881.8	400	181.4
41.9	19	8.6	99.2	45	20.4	1102.3	500	226.8
44.1	20	9.1	101.4	46	20.9	1322.8	600	272.2
46.3	21	9.5	103.6	47	21.3	1543.2	700	317.5
48.5	22	10.0	105.8	48	21.8	1653.5	750	340.2
50.7	23	10.4	108.0	49	22.2	1763.7	800	362.9
52.9	24	10.9	110.2	50	22.7	1984.2	900	408.2
55.1	25	11.3	121.3	55	24.9	2204.6	1000	453.6
57.3	26	11.8	132.3	60	27.2			

WEIGHT CONVERSION TABLE: OUNCES/GRAMS

Oz x 28.34952 = Gm   Gm x 0.03527 = Oz

Oz	Known	Gm	Oz	Known	Gm
			0.99	28	793.8
0.001	1/64 (.016)	0.5	1.02	29	822.1
0.002	1/16 (.063)	1.8	1.06	30	850.5
0.004	1/8 (.125)	3.5	1.2	35	992.2
0.009	1/4 (.250)	7.1	1.4	40	1134.0
0.013	3/8 (.375)	10.6	1.6	45	1275.7
0.018	1/2 (.500)	14.2	1.8	50	1417.5
0.022	5/8 (.625)	17.7	1.9	55	1559.2
0.026	3/4 (.750)	21.3	2.1	60	1701.0
0.031	7/8 (.875)	24.8	2.3	65	1842.7
0.035	1	28.3	2.5	70	1984.5
0.07	2	56.7	2.6	75	2126.2
0.11	3	85.0	2.8	80	2268.0
0.14	4	113.4	3.0	85	2409.7
0.18	5	141.7	3.2	90	2551.5
0.21	6	170.1	3.4	95	2693.2
0.25	7	198.4	3.5	100	2835.0
0.28	8	226.8	3.9	110	3118.4
0.32	9	255.1	4.2	120	3401.9
0.35	10	283.5	4.4	125	3543.7
0.39	11	311.8	4.6	130	3685.4
0.42	12	340.2	4.9	140	3968.9
0.46	13	368.5	5.3	150	4252.4
0.49	14	396.9	6.2	175	4961.2
0.53	15	425.2	7.1	200	5670.0
0.56	16	453.6	7.9	225	6378.7
0.60	17	481.9	8.8	250	7087.4
0.63	18	510.3	9.7	275	7796.1
0.67	19	538.6	10.6	300	8504.9
0.71	20	567.0	11.5	325	9213.6
0.74	21	595.3	12.3	350	9922.3
0.78	22	623.7	13.2	375	10631.1
0.81	23	652.0	14.1	400	11339.8
0.85	24	680.4	15.0	425	12048.5
0.88	25	708.7	15.9	450	12757.3
0.92	26	737.1	16.8	475	13466.0
0.95	27	765.4	17.6	500	14174.8

LENGTH CONVERSION TABLE: INCHES/CENTIMETERS

In × 2.54 = Cm   Cm × 0.3937008 = In

In	Known	Cm	In	Known	Cm
0.05	⅛ (0.13)	0.3	6.3	16	40.6
0.10	¼ (0.25)	0.6	6.7	17	43.2
0.13	⅓ (0.33)	0.8	7.1	18	45.7
0.20	½ (0.50)	1.2	7.5	19	48.3
0.26	⅔ (0.67)	1.7	7.9	20	50.8
0.3	¾ (0.75)	1.9	8.3	21	53.3
0.4	1	2.5	8.7	22	55.9
0.8	2	5.1	9.1	23	58.4
1.2	3	7.6	9.4	24	61.0
1.6	4	10.2	9.8	25	63.5
2.0	5	12.7	10.2	26	66.0
2.4	6	15.2	10.6	27	68.6
2.8	7	17.8	11.0	28	71.1
3.2	8	20.3	11.4	29	73.7
3.5	9	22.9	11.8	30	76.2
3.9	10	25.4	12.2	31	78.7
4.3	11	27.9	12.6	32	81.3
4.7	12	30.5	13.0	33	83.8
5.1	13	33.0	13.4	34	86.4
5.5	14	35.6	13.8	35	88.9
5.9	15	38.1	14.2	36	91.4

LENGTH CONVERSION TABLE: FEET/METERS

Ft × 0.3048 = M   M × 3.28084 = Ft

Ft	Known	M	Ft	Known	M
0.8	¼ (0.25)	0.08	45.9	14	4.3
1.1	⅓ (0.33)	0.10	49.2	15	4.6
1.6	½ (0.50)	0.15	52.5	16	4.9
2.2	⅔ (0.67)	0.20	55.8	17	5.2
2.5	¾ (0.75)	0.23	59.1	18	5.5
3.3	1	0.3	62.3	19	5.8
6.6	2	0.6	65.6	20	6.1
9.8	3	0.9	68.9	21	6.4
13.1	4	1.2	72.2	22	6.7
16.4	5	1.5	75.5	23	7.0
19.7	6	1.8	78.7	24	7.3
23.0	7	2.1	82.0	25	7.6
26.3	8	2.4	85.3	26	7.9
29.6	9	2.7	88.6	27	8.2
32.8	10	3.0	91.9	28	8.5
36.1	11	3.4	95.1	29	8.8
39.4	12	3.7	98.4	30	9.1
42.7	13	4.0			

LENGTH AND DISTANCE CONVERSION TABLE: YARDS/METERS

Yd × 0.9144 = M   M × 1.093613 = Yd

Yd	Known	M	Yd	Known	M	Yd	Known	M
0.3	¼ (0.25)	0.2	21.9	20	18.3	382.8	350	320.0
0.4	⅓ (0.33)	0.3	27.3	25	22.9	437.4	400	365.8
0.55	½ (0.50)	0.46	32.8	30	27.4	492.1	450	411.5
0.7	⅔ (0.67)	0.6	43.7	40	36.6	546.8	500	457.2
0.8	¾ (0.75)	0.7	54.7	50	45.7	656.2	600	548.6
1.1	1	0.9	65.6	60	54.9	765.5	700	640.1
2.2	2	1.8	76.6	70	64.0	820.2	750	685.8
3.3	3	2.7	87.5	80	73.2	874.9	800	731.5
4.4	4	3.7	98.4	90	82.3	984.3	900	823.0
5.5	5	4.6	109.4	100	91.4	1093.6	1000	914.4
6.6	6	5.5	136.7	125	114.3	1312.3	1200	1097.3
7.7	7	6.4	164.0	150	137.2	1640.4	1500	1371.6
8.8	8	7.3	191.4	175	160.0	2187.2	2000	1828.8
9.9	9	8.2	218.7	200	182.9	2734.0	2500	2286.0
10.9	10	9.1	273.4	250	228.6	3280.8	3000	2743.2
16.4	15	13.7	328.1	300	274.3	5468.1	5000	4572.0

DISTANCE AND SPEED CONVERSION TABLE: MILES/KILOMETERS (MPH/KPH)

Mi (or mph) × 1.6093 = Km (or kph)   Km (or kph) × 0.62137 = Mi (or mph)

Mi (mph)	Known	Km (kph)	Mi (mph)	Known	Km (kph)	Mi (mph)	Known	Km (kph)
0.16	¼ (0.25)	0.4	8.1	13	20.9	21.7	35	56.3
0.2	⅓ (0.33)	0.5	8.7	14	22.5	24.9	40	64.4
0.3	½ (0.50)	0.8	9.3	15	24.1	28.0	45	72.4
0.4	⅔ (0.67)	1.1	9.9	16	25.7	31.1	50	80.5
0.5	¾ (0.75)	1.2	10.6	17	27.4	37.3	60	96.6
0.6	1	1.6	11.2	18	29.0	43.5	70	112.6
1.2	2	3.2	11.8	19	30.6	46.6	75	120.7
1.9	3	4.8	12.4	20	32.2	49.7	80	128.7
2.5	4	6.4	13.0	21	33.8	55.9	90	144.8
3.1	5	8.0	13.7	22	35.4	62.1	100	160.9
3.7	6	9.7	14.3	23	37.0	77.7	125	201.2
4.3	7	11.3	14.9	24	38.6	93.2	150	241.4
5.0	8	12.9	15.5	25	40.2	108.7	175	281.6
5.6	9	14.5	16.2	26	41.8	124.3	200	321.9
6.2	10	16.1	16.8	27	43.5	155.3	250	402.3
6.8	11	17.7	17.4	28	45.1	186.4	300	482.8
7.5	12	19.3	18.0	29	46.7	310.7	500	804.7
			18.6	30	48.3			

DISTANCE AND SPEED CONVERSION TABLE: NAUTICAL MILES/KILOMETERS (KNOTS/KPH)

$$Nm \text{ (or kt)} \times 1.852 = Km \text{ (or kph)}$$
$$Km \text{ (or kph)} \times 0.54 = Nm \text{ (or kt)}$$

Nm (kt)	Known	Km (kph)	Nm (kt)	Known	Km (kph)
0.1	¼ (0.25)	0.5	11.9	22	40.7
0.2	⅓ (0.33)	0.6	12.4	23	42.6
0.3	½ (0.50)	0.9	13.0	24	44.4
0.36	⅔ (0.67)	1.2	13.5	25	46.3
0.41	¾ (0.75)	1.4	14.0	26	48.2
0.5	1	1.9	14.6	27	50.0
1.1	2	3.7	15.1	28	51.9
1.6	3	5.6	15.7	29	53.7
2.2	4	7.4	16.2	30	55.6
2.7	5	9.3	18.9	35	64.8
3.2	6	11.1	21.6	40	74.1
3.8	7	13.0	24.3	45	83.3
4.3	8	14.8	27.0	50	92.6
4.9	9	16.7	32.4	60	111.1
5.4	10	18.5	37.8	70	129.6
5.9	11	20.4	40.5	75	138.9
6.5	12	22.2	43.2	80	148.2
7.0	13	24.1	48.6	90	166.7
7.6	14	26.0	54.0	100	185.2
8.1	15	27.8	67.5	125	231.5
8.6	16	29.6	81.0	150	277.8
9.2	17	31.5	94.5	175	324.1
9.7	18	33.3	108.0	200	370.4
10.3	19	35.2	135.0	250	463.0
10.8	20	37.0	162.0	300	555.6
11.3	21	38.9	270.0	500	926.0

DISTANCE AND SPEED CONVERSION TABLE: MILES/NAUTICAL MILES (MPH/KNOTS)

Mi (or mph) × 0.869 = Nm (or kt)

Nm (or kt) × 1.1508 = Mi (or mph)

Mi (mph)	Known	Nm (kt)	Mi (mph)	Known	Nm (kt)
0.3	¼ (0.25)	0.2	25.3	22	19.1
0.4	⅓ (0.33)	0.3	26.5	23	20.0
0.6	½ (0.50)	0.4	27.6	24	20.9
0.8	⅔ (0.67)	0.6	28.8	25	21.7
0.9	¾ (0.75)	0.7	29.9	26	22.6
1.2	1	0.9	31.1	27	23.5
2.3	2	1.7	32.2	28	24.3
3.5	3	2.6	33.4	29	25.2
4.6	4	3.5	34.5	30	26.1
5.8	5	4.3	40.3	35	30.4
6.9	6	5.2	46.0	40	34.8
8.1	7	6.1	51.8	45	39.1
9.2	8	7.0	57.5	50	43.5
10.4	9	7.8	69.0	60	52.1
11.5	10	8.7	80.6	70	60.8
12.7	11	9.6	86.3	75	65.2
13.8	12	10.4	92.1	80	69.5
15.0	13	11.3	103.6	90	78.2
16.1	14	12.2	115.1	100	86.9
17.3	15	13.0	143.9	125	108.6
18.4	16	13.9	172.6	150	130.4
19.6	17	14.8	201.4	175	152.1
20.7	18	15.6	230.2	200	173.8
21.9	19	16.5	287.7	250	217.3
23.0	20	17.4	345.2	300	260.7
24.2	21	18.2	575.4	500	434.5

INDEX